T0306183

THE LAWYER'S GUIDE TO BUSINESS ETHICS

Legal practice is both a profession and, increasingly, a business. Lawyers are routinely confronted with a complex set of ethical questions due to the adversarial nature of legal practice and justice, and at the same time handle relationships with different stakeholders within their own practice, including clients, partners, and managers. This presents a unique set of challenges that are not experienced in other professions. This book provides a framework to guide the practicing lawyer through these various levels of ethical complexity.

Written in a highly accessible style, *The Lawyer's Guide to Business Ethics* transforms business ethics theory for the practice of law, identifying the unique applications and ways in which lawyers can utilize the theory and principles to enhance their decision making and case management techniques. The book examines the social, ethical, personal, and economic forces influencing lawyers' work, explains the rules of professional conduct, and presents real-life ethical dilemmas to enhance learning and to assist in finding appropriate outcomes.

This book will be an invaluable resource for legal practitioners, law students and business students, and anyone interested in maintaining ethical behavior in the practice of law.

Keith William Diener is a tenured Associate Professor at Stockton University where he teaches courses in law and ethics. He holds two doctoral degrees, in law and business ethics, and two masters' degrees, in international law and philosophy, from Georgetown University, Georgia State University, and George Washington University. He previously held visiting positions at the George Washington University and the Universidad de La Salle, and an Adjunct Professorship at the University of Maryland, Global Campus. Dr. Diener has published extensively on legal and ethical issues and received numerous research awards from national and international law and ethics organizations. He is a licensed practicing attorney in New Jersey, North Carolina, Virginia, and the District of Columbia.

Giving Voice to Values

Series Editor: Mary C. Gentile

The *Giving Voice to Values* series is a collection of books on Business Ethics and Corporate Social Responsibility that brings a practical, solutions-oriented, skill-building approach to the salient questions of values-driven leadership.

Giving Voice to Values (GVV: www.GivingVoiceToValues.org) – the curriculum, the pedagogy and the research upon which it is based – was designed to transform the foundational assumptions upon which the teaching of business ethics is based, and importantly, to equip future business leaders to know not only what is right – but how to make it happen.

Engaging the Heart in Business
Alice Alessandri and Alberto Aleo

Shaping the Future of Work
A Handbook for Building a New Social Contract
Thomas A. Kochan and Lee Dyer

Professionalism and Values in Law Practice
Robert Feldman

Giving Voice to Values in the Boardroom
Cynthia E. Clark

Giving Voice to Values
An Innovation and Impact Agenda
Jerry Goodstein and Mary C. Gentile

Collaborating for Climate Resilience
Ann Goodman and Nilda M. Mesa

Tactics for Racial Justice
Building an Antiracist Organization and Community
Shannon Joyce Prince

The Lawyer's Guide to Business Ethics
Keith William Diener

For more information about this series, please visit: www.routledge.com/Giving-Voice-to-Values/book-series/GVV

THE LAWYER'S GUIDE TO BUSINESS ETHICS

Keith William Diener

Routledge
Taylor & Francis Group

LONDON AND NEW YORK

Cover image: Getty Images

First published 2023
by Routledge
4 Park Square, Milton Park, Abingdon, Oxon OX14 4RN

and by Routledge
605 Third Avenue, New York, NY 10158

Routledge is an imprint of the Taylor & Francis Group, an informa business

British Library Cataloguing-in-Publication Data
A catalogue record for this book is available from the British Library

Library of Congress Cataloging-in-Publication Data
Names: Diener, Keith William, author.
Title: The lawyer's guide to business ethics / Keith William Diener.
Description: Milton Park, Abingdon, Oxon ; New York, NY : Routledge, 2023. |
Series: Giving voice to values, 2578-5060 | Includes bibliographical references
and index.
Subjects: LCSH: Business ethics. | Legal ethics. | Commercial law.
Classification: LCC HF5387 .D53 2023 (print) | LCC HF5387 (ebook) |
DDC 174/.4—dc23/eng/20220523
LC record available at https://lccn.loc.gov/2022022544
LC ebook record available at https://lccn.loc.gov/2022022545

ISBN: 978-1-138-54974-6 (hbk)
ISBN: 978-1-138-54973-9 (pbk)
ISBN: 978-0-429-50784-7 (ebk)

DOI: 10.4324/9780429507847

Typeset in Joanna
by codeMantra

For my son

CONTENTS

PREFACE

This book was written because the world today is full of people who engage in unethical conduct. This book was written because the world today is full of people who engage in ethical conduct. At one time or another, we've all fallen into both categories. In other words, we've all engaged in behaviors that are ethical and unethical at some point in our lives, regardless of the theory or measure of ethics one prescribes to. Yet only some of us consistently desire to do the right thing and consciously examine our actions and intentions to strive to engage in ethical behavior.

This book is written primarily for those attorneys who desire to do the right thing. Its aim is to provide tools, many rooted in contemporary business ethics theory, to aid those attorneys with effectively voicing their values in legal contexts while simultaneously strategically attempting to mitigate potential fall-out from doing so. The task of this book involves appealing to language and principles that are far from a perfect science. The ideas set forth in this book should be perceived as a "guide" which may be deviated from and modified as the circumstances require. If the mission of this book is successful, this guide will eventually be improved upon and expanded by persons much smarter and wiser than this author.

As an exercise in interdisciplinary work, this book pulls from the author's unique background and education in the legal field, business ethics, and academia. This book adapts the work of business ethicists and business ethics theory to the legal profession. In crossing disciplines, there is an inherent risk that language, terminology, and practices of one field may not coincide with similar understandings in another field. Simultaneously, although some confusion may arise, there is greater potential that such differences may lead to an enhanced understanding and advancement across disciplines. Those with background in what philosophers refer to as "normative" business ethics may best understand how the use of language in a discipline may be contradicted by use of the same language in another discipline. Learned psychologists may similarly understand this point. Any mistakes are my own.

Dr. Keith William Diener, Esq.

INTRODUCTION

The Lawyer's Guide to Business Ethics explores how lawyers can engage in ethical practices including and beyond complying with professional rules. This book takes business ethics theory and transplants it into the legal profession, determining in the process, that there is much that legal practitioners can take from business ethics theory and even more that attorneys can utilize to enhance their decision making and case management techniques. The book unfolds in three parts.

Part I traces the historical development of the contemporary common law legal system. It describes salient environmental factors that influence ethics in the legal field. It begins in Chapter 1 by tracing the history of the common law to decipher the historical roots of norms in legal practice, revealing that the legal field has a history fraught with practices that deviate from general societal norms. The contemporary legal landscape in the United States is a product of over a millennium of historical events that have created an imperfect institution for administering justice. The U.S. system diverged in many ways from its English roots as it developed many of its

DOI: 10.4324/9780429507847-1

own legal norms that now deviate from its birth mother. Chapter 2 examines how the American Rule on the recovery of attorneys' fees, one such norm, has influenced the evolution of the practice of law in the United States including the progression of entrepreneurial litigation. Chapter 3 then examines the impact of the economy on the practice of law and examines how broader socio-economic trends can impact and influence the practice of law and the motivations and needs of attorneys. Part I is intended to describe the central aspects of the external political and economic systems within which attorneys in the United States are currently working and how this system may influence ethical decision making.

With the broader context set forth, Part II turns to the individual legal practitioner who works in the contemporary legal environment. Chapter 4 examines the role of the attorney as an advocate and the core values of advocacy. These values are defined and explored in the context of the adversarial setting of the practice of law. The strategies of *Giving Voice to Values* are examined and implemented to decipher ways of expressing values effectively in legal contexts. Chapter 4, and each chapter after, contains illustrative scenarios which reveal how the strategies of *Giving Voice to Values* may be applied within the legal field.[1] Chapter 5 turns to the attorney's challenge of building trust with stakeholders and adapts Fort's tripartite vision of trust to the practice of law. Developing trust with clients and other stakeholders is a key component of effective advocacy. Following the examination of trust, Chapter 6 investigates the unethical employer and firm environment. It provides an outline of a process for subordinates who desire to address unethical and unprofessional conduct of their superiors in firm settings, giving due consideration to legal and ethical concerns. Part II is aimed at examining the attorney's role as an advocate and how that role can be enhanced by adherence to values.

Having considered the external environment and the role of the attorney as an advocate, Part III delves deeper into ways that attorneys can effectively voice their values in legal practice by moving beyond the strict letter of the rules of professional conduct. Chapter 7 examines the professional rules and how values can play a role in promoting ethical action beyond mere compliance. Chapter 8 adapts the stakeholder concept from business ethics literature to the legal profession and discusses how the concept and theory may provide both instrumental and normative insights to practitioners. Chapter 9 considers that law has business components that cannot be separated from people and ethics. It suggests that the social contract needs to be modified to exclude extreme profit-seeking motivations from the legal field, and that embedding virtues and values into the education, profession, and practice of law, and implementing the strategies of *Giving Voice to Values* will over time contribute to overcoming rationalizations. Part III is intended to motivate attorneys to look to and beyond the model rules when making practice decisions.

The three parts combine to form an introductory guide to how the theory and principles of business ethics, including the tenets of *Giving Voice to Values*, may be utilized to improve ethical decision making in the legal field.

Note

1 Most of the illustrative scenarios are composites that are pulled from the author's years of legal practice experience, and others are fictional examples. The author made every effort to maintain anonymity in all illustrative scenarios by changing names, places, details, and facts to such a considerable degree that there should not be any resemblance to actual persons or events. The illustrations are intended to reveal how the *Giving Voice to Values* strategies and theory discussed in this book may be implemented. Each situation is unique, and the context of the situation, values, local professional rules, laws, and other environment factors should be considered before implementing any strategy.

Part I

THE RISE OF THE CONTEMPORARY LEGAL LANDSCAPE

Part I traces the historical development of the contemporary common law legal system by examining salient environmental factors that influence ethics in the legal field. This Part begins by tracing the history of the common law to decipher the historical roots of norms in legal practice, revealing that the legal field has a history fraught with practices that deviate from general societal norms. The contemporary legal landscape in the United States is a product of over a millennium of historical events that have created an imperfect institution for administering justice. The U.S. system diverged in many ways from its English roots as it developed many of its own legal norms that now deviate from its birth mother. The American Rule on the recovery of attorneys' fees is one such norm that has influenced the evolution of the practice of law in the United States including the progression of entrepreneurial litigation. This Part then examines the impact of the economy on the practice of law and how broader socio-economic trends

DOI: 10.4324/9780429507847-2

can impact and influence the practice of law and the motivations and needs of attorneys. Part I is intended to describe the central aspects of the external political and economic systems within which attorneys in the United States are currently working and how this system may influence ethical decision making.

1

THE RISE OF THE ADVERSARIAL SYSTEM

The common law system is adversarial, many people say. Advocates zealously argue cases on behalf of their clients and the outcome rendered is deemed institutional justice. But there are many who say the adversarial system is unfair and does not always establish justice. Attorneys are criticized as unethical, and yet are expected to win cases for clients. It is quipped that "lawsuits are war ... and they all begin the same way – with a declaration of war: the complaint."[1] In war, people are killed but this killing isn't considered murder. In lawsuits, people are harmed but this harm isn't considered illegal. Skilled attorneys weaponize and leverage the rules of professional conduct and court to win the war, often without regard to the generally accepted moral norms of society or the proverbial "spirit of the law." Some claim that attorneys should both win cases within the rules of the system and abide by society's moral norms – ignoring the apparent inconsistency. One way of attempting to reconcile this apparent inconsistency is to trace the history of the adversarial system to decipher the role of societal moral norms in it across time. Throughout the history of the adversarial system,

DOI: 10.4324/9780429507847-3

those involved have been granted considerable concessions to engage in behaviors that do not cohere with the moral norms of the rest of society.

History of the Adversarial System

Many legal scholars and historians trace the contemporary adversarial system's genesis to the "trial by battle," a practice that persisted during the Middle Ages in Europe and appeared most certainly in Britain following the Norman conquest of 1066. The trial by battle required the participants (or their champions) to physically combat each other until one party yielded, was defeated, or, in more serious cases, was killed. The trial was overseen by a judicial officer, and solemn oaths were required before engaging in combat. Some scholars suggest that these trials by battle were the beginning of the adversarial system, but others point to the alternatives available in England during this time, including the trial by ordeal and the wager of law.[2] The trial by ordeal involved spiritual tests such as holding a hot iron bar, pulling a stone from a pot of boiling water, or even tying up an accused and throwing the accused into a lake. If innocent, the accused would swiftly heal from the burn, or would sink in the lake. The innocence depended on God's intervention.[3] The wager of law was essentially a test of character where the accused would swear to innocence and others, often referred to as compurgators, would testify as to the accused's character.[4] While early Germanic peoples were said to endorse the blood feud as the means of resolving disputes, and that "early forms of legal procedure were grounded in vengeance,"[5] over time, a much more sophisticated and nuanced approach to dispute resolution emerged from these early gestations of justice.

The Norman conquest, led by William the Conqueror, brought with it an increasing use of the French language in British legal contexts. The French-speaking Normans conquered the English-speaking Saxons. This led to more French entering the language of the common law. Mellinkoff suggests that the tale that William's conquest caused a complete turn to French in the British courts is a myth.[6] Historical evidence suggests that Latin and English were the primary languages of the written law after the conquest, and even that William tried to master the English language. Nevertheless, the French language seeped deeper into the English common law system over the centuries after the Norman conquest.[7] Consequently, when American colonists brought the common law with them across the pond, it was filled with French words that remain in the vocabulary of American lawyers today.[8] A "tort," for instance, literally translated from the French is a "wrong" or "injury" and these wrongs have become a vital component of civil law within the American common law system.[9] The vocabulary and practices of the common law are an historical amalgamation of language, culture, and social conventions that have evolved over time.[10]

Prior to the Norman period, the law in England remained largely consuetudinary. The customs and primitive codes of the Saxons were mostly customary but with smattered influence from Roman law and Scripture. The customs were diverse and established in local folk courts, without presiding professional judges, and were given the force of contemporary positive law in each region. During the reign of William the Conqueror, the Saxon folk courts remained in play, and were joined by the manor courts of the Norman barons, together serving as courts of first resort for the local populations.[11] As one commentator explains,

> [t]hese courts, made up of a considerable body of men fairly representative of the average of the people, uneducated and entirely lacking in anything like legal knowledge or training in the modern sense, administered an extremely rude kind of law, unwritten, made up of the customs of the people, varying from time to time and in different communities, and handed down from generation to generation by word of mouth. The forms of trial were, for the most part, appeals to the supernatural.[12]

Over time, however, these courts fell into disuse as more formalized courts were established. Among them, William established the *Curia Regis*, or King's Court, which was, at that time, composed of a body of barons, ecclesiastics, and a Chief Justiciary to preside over disputes. At that time, the *Curia Regis* was granted broad legislative, judicial, and administrative powers. William also appointed itinerant justices to travel to and preside over disputes in various counties. These developments formed the basis for the contemporary courts of the common law legal system, including the professional judges that preside over them.[13]

Through subsequent monarchs, the King's Court and itinerant justices continued to be used. The King's Court was increasingly utilized and eventually, under Henry II (twelfth century), its judicial function was separated from its legislative function. Henry II's establishment of a national court, invention of new writs, and trial by juries instead of by battle or other means was a major step in the progression toward the contemporary common law system. Henry II's reforms led to a national law in England and a centralized court system with professional judges presiding over circuits which were composed of multiple neighboring counties. Ecclesiastical courts, even at this time, had the power to hear questions of marriage, wills, and other disputes involving ecclesiastical questions. The ecclesiastical courts were, however, prohibited from interfering in other issues.[14] Henry II's centralization of courts was not without its critics. His reform took powers away from the barons and reserved those powers to the King. Henry II's son, King John was compelled to grant the original Magna Carta in 1215, in part, because of Henry II's reforms, and in part, because John increased taxes on barons and acted dishonorably. The Magna Carta, which has become a symbol of liberty, stands for the principle that the King is subject to law and, further, gives freemen the right to trial before imprisonment. Albeit Pope Innocent III declared the Magna Carta null and void only months after its granting, it was revised and reissued numerous times in the century that followed.[15]

Even prior to the time of Henry II, skilled defendants could utilize the rules of court to their benefit. In the King's Court, the suit began with a writ, which was served by a sheriff, and could be enforced by a seizure of defendant's land. For a period, the essoin could be used, much like a continuance, to delay or prolong proceedings on a writ of right for years. Strategic defendants could utilize these delays for their benefit, but under Henry II, the use of essoins was limited and judgments more swiftly made.[16]

Meanwhile, the official birth of magistrate courts came when Edward I (thirteenth century) commissioned "good and lawful men" to keep the peace.[17] From that point forward, Justices of the Peace have played an essential role in the English judicial system. Yet, the interlinking of politics and the judiciary often created problems. For years, Edward III's Chancellors also served as common law judges.[18] The exact historical timeline is hazy, but it is apparent that during this period, and certainly by the time of Edward III (fourteenth century), the Court of Chancery was a regular tribunal that administered equitable remedies based on the guiding principles of honesty, equity, and conscience.[19] However, equity was utilized in various ways and by various instruments of justice long before the formal establishment of the Court of Chancery.[20]

By the seventeenth century, the interlinking of politics and the judiciary led to presiding judges coercing juries. Presiding judges threatened, starved, and locked juries up until they reached the verdicts desired by the bench.[21] The principle of jury independence began to develop particularly after the trial of Penn and Mead.[22] The jurors in this case were threatened if they did not return the desired verdict, but they refused to enter the verdict desired by the judges.[23] Sir Thomas Howell, who tried the case, exclaimed that "Gentlemen, you shall not be dismissed till you bring in a verdict which the court will accept. You shall be locked up, without meat, drink, fire, and tobacco."[24] The judges, after several attempts to persuade the jury to find Penn and Mead guilty, fined the jurors for contempt and locked them away until their fines were paid. The jurors subsequently petitioned the court of Common Pleas for a writ of habeas corpus. After much suffering, the justices unanimously "ruled that the jury had been illegally fined and imprisoned and that a jury could not be punished for its verdict."[25] This decision paved the way for increasing impartiality and independence of jurors – an essential component of a fair trial within the adversarial system.

The range of adversarial mechanisms expanded and refined over the following century and by the end of the eighteenth century, the adversarial system was robustly established both in England and America.[26] The courts of equity remained separate courts in England until the English Judicature Act, with similar reforms by many of the American states occurring in the nineteenth century. The reforms largely combined the courts of law and equity into one forum where either remedy could be attained.[27] The English Judicature Act created the Supreme Court of Judicature and abolished many of the courts that had been in effect since the Middle Ages. The Supreme Court of Judicature included the Court of Appeal and High Court of Justice (with its five branches) and continued to be refined in the years that followed the Act.[28] It continued progress toward modernization of the common law court system, which underwent another major reform in the twentieth century with the establishment of the Crown Courts.

Meanwhile, a rights revolution began in the centuries that followed Edward III, as influential philosophers like Thomas Hobbes and John Locke penned their rights-grounded social contract theories.[29] Locke's theory is believed to have played a pivotal role in establishing rights such as those found in the American Declaration of Independence (1776).[30] Locke's theories of natural rights, including life, liberty, and property, along with his theories of secularization played an immeasurable role in the early development of the American government.[31]

The early American colonial courts brought with them the English common law, which was developed through various conquests, social shifts, reformations, and other evolutionary changes. With the common law came the continued adherence to the adversarial system of law in America. Over time, the 50 states developed their systems for the governance of state law issues, and the federal government developed its federal court system, with the U.S. Supreme Court as the court of last resort. The 50 state systems, however, were not solely influenced by the English common law but different regions were influenced by the various colonies that occupied their territories. For instance, Louisiana's preservation of the French civil law and anomalies in Texas and California reflect their colonized roots.[32] Yet, the common law adversarial system has largely overtaken America and other former British colonies today.[33] Its essential features merit attention.

Characteristics of the Adversarial System

The characteristics of the contemporary adversarial system are the product of more than a millennium of evolution. Adversarial systems exist in many realms of society including sports, business, games, politics, and law. The essential characteristics of the common law adversarial system, sometimes called the "adversary system" or herein the "adversarial system," include competing adversaries who are often represented by advocates, a focus on winning within the applicable rules, detailed procedural requirements, role responsibilities of those working within the system, a limited potential for collaboration between adversaries, and impartial decision makers (judges/juries). This system assumes that a competitive process is a suitable mechanism for ensuring justice is achieved, the "fundamental purpose" of which "is the ascertainment of the truth with respect, most frequently, to an event which took place in the past."[34]

Adversaries, often represented by advocates, are responsible for bringing evidence before a judge, and presenting that evidence in a way that most benefits their respective arguments. These advocates play a substantial role in the fact-finding process, through the discovery mechanisms that are authorized by court rules. They engage in confrontational and accusatorial practices aimed at benefiting their side and are motivated by self-interest to win. Talented advocates tell the story of their clients by creating narrative versions of the facts, as supported by evidence. Advocates are, in contemporary times, increasingly necessary to navigate the procedural hurdles faced by litigants.

The advocate's aim is usually to win the case by utilizing procedural rules and narratives as necessary to achieve this result. These procedural rules, including burdens of proof, play an integral role in the conduct and presentation of the litigation process. The rules of court, such as the Federal Rules of Civil Procedure and local rules, govern the timeliness, practices, and methods of the court. Other procedural limitations, such as the statute of limitations and exhaustion of administrative remedies, are typically governed by statutes and regulations. A failure to strictly adhere to procedural requirements can lead to the loss of a case regardless of its merits. The varying procedures and beyond procedures, the informal conventions of U.S. courts, pose particularly difficult queries for advocates. The way a case proceeds through the system in the county court of one state can be quite different across counties in the same state, and substantially different in other states' courts. Advocates are burdened with the complicated task of familiarizing themselves with the local procedures and customs of each court in which they appear. Trial does not always result in the party that deserves to win prevailing, but rather some procedure or other rule of the forum may lead to a default or technical loss despite the merits of the case. To the extent that the adversarial system is intended to establish justice, it often fails in that regard.

As representatives, advocates are subject to certain conflicts, including conflicting salient moral descriptions.[35] These conflicts arise from the role of the advocate in the adversarial system, and the duties of an advocate, along with the rights granted to an advocate within this institutional system. As described below, it is not uncommon for the duties of an advocate to conflict with duties that an individual, outside of the adversarial system, may have as a human being thriving in society who, beyond an advocate, is also a family member, colleague, friend, or acquaintance. The outspoken advocate with a skill for distinguishing meaning and technicalities in the context of legal argumentation is highly valued in litigation contexts. While valued in one's role as an advocate, these same skills can be destructive if overused outside of one's role as an advocate such as in personal disagreements or relationship contexts.

In personal disagreements, cooperating and understanding the other are essential to maintaining functional long-term relationships. Yet, in adversarial contexts, the ability to cooperate and seek mutual understanding is limited. Alternative dispute resolution (ADR) mechanisms, such as mediation and conciliation, provide institutionally acceptable methods for cooperating within adversarial contexts. ADR exists within the broader adversarial context, and the roles of adversaries are perpetuated but placed in a context aimed at facilitating a resolution to a dispute. Certain ADR processes, such as arbitration, bear many resemblances to trials, while mediation and conciliation to a lesser extent perpetuate the "conflicting sides" of a dispute and are sometimes leveraged as discovery tools, to prolong proceedings, or for other bad faith reasons.

Advocates in the adversarial environment often utilize guised cooperation to their benefit. This strategy is available to advocates, whose ethical limitations are broadly fixed by rules of professional conduct. The rules of professional conduct, like other kinds of professional codes, are aimed at providing a baseline understanding of the limits of proper conduct, but, like other types of codes, often are utilized as a grant of permission to engage in activities that are not prohibited by the rules. As discussed further in Chapter 7, advocates do weaponize the rules of professional conduct as both swords and shields and such abuses are unfortunately contagious, insomuch as once a practice is normalized, attorneys may fear that failing to engage in that practice could lead to disadvantage. Therefore, the boards overseeing the rules of professional conduct are essential to regulation within and outside of trial processes. They place the outermost limit on permissible conduct in adversarial settings.

Within the trial process of an adversarial system, the judge plays the primary role of controlling the trial, ensuring the procedures are followed, and, to some extent, safeguarding a just outcome. Mandated impartiality is inherent to the role of the judiciary in adversarial settings, but absolute impartiality is an unattainable ideal as political ideologies, moral inclinations, and inherent personal biases inevitably bleed into the decisions of judges. The "living" nature of the law allows for judges in common law systems to interpret and even create standards not envisioned or expressly stated in legislation. There are both benefits and downsides to the broad powers allocated to judges, including the potential for enforcing or abusing the lex non scripta of a given time. An impartial jury is similarly essential to justice, but juries too have their inherent biases and prejudices which creep into verdicts.

The preceding characteristics, despite the proffered weaknesses, retain many strengths that are intended to provide adversaries with a fair and unbiased hearing. The adversarial system itself is often compared to inquisitorial civil law systems that have evolved from Roman law, and generally differ insofar as they maintain stricter adherence to codes, downplay or eliminate the role of precedent, downplay the role of advocates instead in favor of an increased fact-finding function by the court, and more empowered judges. Some commentators believe the inquisitorial system as an overall better, more sophisticated, and civilized system. The common law adversarial system is not without its critics, and these criticisms merit attention.

Criticisms of Adversarial System

It should be of little surprise that there are criticisms of the adversarial system. It does, after all, entail competitive trials, each of which renders a winner and a loser. Roughly half of all participants in trials are losers who often rationalize their losses by appealing to notions that the system is "rigged" or "corrupt." Even those who win cases often complain about the costs of winning, both monetary (e.g., attorneys' fees) and non-monetary (e.g., opportunity and psychological costs). Aside from features that cannot be avoided, such as fading or inaccurate human memory, which can lead to problems with trials, particularly when witnesses forget details or are mistaken in their conflicting memories of events, there are at least three other interrelated criticisms of the adversarial system. The first is that the legal system has become a culture of gamesmanship. The second is that disparate resources impact outcomes. The third is that lawyers are unethical. These three criticisms are perennial problems. Former Chief Justice of the U.S. Supreme Court Warren E. Burger identified these shortcomings of American practice in the 1970s.[36] They remain criticisms of the adversarial system today.

In the 1970s, Justice Burger asserted that "after more than 35 years' experience with pretrial procedures, we hear widespread complaints that they are being misused and overused. Increasingly in the past 20 years, responsible lawyers have pointed to abuses of the pretrial processes in civil cases."[37] This element of "sporting" or "gamesmanship" has long been a criticism of the adversarial system. To begin with an example of such gamesmanship, a common attorney strategy is to create a burdensome amount of work to wear the other side down. This is especially prevalent in litigation contexts when one side maintains significantly more resources than the other and can put a cadre of attorneys to work on a single case. This cadre may object to providing information in discovery, leading to a song-and-dance of letters, meet and confers, and motions to compel by the requestor, until finally, at the last moment possible, the information requested is provided, but only after the requestor has expended considerable time and resources attempting to get what should have been provided in the first place.[38] While the requestor is burdened with preparing for the motion to compel, other members of the cadre are stealthily working behind the scenes on a dispositive motion which will soon be strategically filed at the most inconvenient time for the requestor. If the case survives this motion, the cadre may then request mediation without any intention whatsoever of settling the case, but instead, to utilize the carrot of mediation to wear down the other side's resources, only to then to be whacked with the stick of an irrationally low settlement offer.

As the preceding example illustrates, the norms of an adversarial system, much like the rules of a sport or a game, can seem antithetical to the values held by society. Few would, outside of the context of litigation, intentionally attempt to wear down and burden another human being to gain an advantage. Similarly, outside of a wrestling match, few would utilize strength and speed to overpower another human being and forcibly hold that person's back to the mat. To win that wrestling match, one must engage in behaviors that would be frowned upon by most in society (or even actions that may be punishable as crimes). Yet, to be a successful wrestler, who is admired and feared by others in the sport, one must consistently defeat one's opponents in accordance with the rules of the sport – no more, no less. One may easily draw parallels between the tactics and strategies of zealous advocates and successful sportsmen and attempt to justify legal strategies based on the "rules of the game." As this argument may go, legal disputes are games of strategy. Not utilizing available resources to advantage one's client by testing the endurance of the opposing party is like releasing one's wrestling opponent from a winning grip out of heartfelt sympathy. Proponents of this view may argue that to do so could contribute to the loss of one's match or greatly reduce one's odds of winning. They may argue that to be a successful lawyer, one must take every opportunity for advantage one can garner within the rules of professional conduct and court – that one must grip one's opponent forcibly and take every opportunity, within the rules of the sport, to throw that opponent to the mat and hold that opponent's back down for the win.

As a player may be penalized for breaking the rules of a game, unfavorable evidence may be left out of a trial, even if that evidence could have helped win the case. In criminal cases, as well, there is considerable room for gamesmanship. As former Justice of the Illinois Supreme Court, Walter Schaefer, stated:

> Here it is that the sporting aspect of the trial becomes most offensive. A defendant has nothing to lose by a succession of attacks upon his judgment of conviction, for if they are successful the result is a vacation of the judgment of conviction with the assurance that upon a retrial he will be no worse off than he is at the time the claim was asserted. There is every incentive therefore to continue the attack even though every means would seem to have been exhausted and the cause hopeless.[39]

The system is set up such that criminals and other losers of trials have everything to gain and little to lose by engaging in creative mechanisms aimed at gaming the system.

The next interrelated criticism of the adversarial system is that parties often have disparate resources available to them. When parties have significantly different financial resources available to them, it often leads to the appearance that money can buy justice. That is, the wealthier party can fight longer and harder than the poorer party by putting oodles of cash into the lawsuit in defense or support of claims. This can be done by paying top-dollar for skilled and experienced attorneys, by engaging in creative litigation techniques, or by pounding the other side, like a raw side of beef, through superfluous motions practices. The outcome of the case will surely be impacted by the skill and experience of attorneys and the resources available to each party. When the money runs out for the poorer party, it may result in that party accepting less than the case is worth, or other miscarriages of justice. The fact that money can drive outcomes of institutional justice is a major shortcoming of the contemporary adversarial system.

"The first thing we do, let's kill all the lawyers" was a line from Shakespeare's *Henry VI*. Some contend that this was an early example of a lawyer joke.[40] Others contend that this line in context was meant to give praise to lawyers, as defenders of justice who stand in the way of corruption.[41] The two interpretations reveal the strange juxtaposition that lawyers maintain in society as both officers of the court and unethical con artists. The complaint that rings as true today as it did in the time of Justice Burger, is that at least some members of the legal profession engage in deceptive and unethical practices. In face of the presence of some unscrupulous attorneys, responsible lawyers must decipher a way of navigating their cases through this system without sacrificing too much of what it means to be human.

Parts II and III of this book provide a roadmap for lawyers navigating this perilous terrain, including strategies and theories intended to provide lawyers the tools they need to act ethically and responsibly even within the most contentious of adversarial contexts. Before turning to these techniques, however, the next couple of chapters will continue exploring the external environment by first, in Chapter 2, analyzing the impact that the American Rule has had on contemporary legal practice and the increase of entrepreneurial litigation, and then, in Chapter 3, by discussing a variety of socio-economic factors that impact contemporary legal practitioners.

Notes

1 *A Civil Action* (Touchstone Pictures 1998).
2 Stephen Landsman, A Brief Survey of the Development of the Adversary System, 44 *Ohio State Law Journal* 713, 717–718 (1983).
3 History of the Judiciary, https://www.judiciary.uk/about-the-judiciary/history-of-the-judiciary/; see also Margaret H. Kerr, Richard D. Forsyth, and Michael J. Plyley, Cold Water and Hot Iron: Trial by Ordeal in England, 22 *Journal of Interdisciplinary History* 573 (1992).
4 Stephen Landsman, A Brief Survey of the Development of the Adversary System, 44 *Ohio State Law Journal* 713, 717–718 (1983).
5 Oliver Wendell Holmes, *The Common Law* (Mark DeWolfe Howe ed., 1963).
6 David Mellinkoff, *The Language of the Law*, 63–70 (1963).
7 *Id.* at 97.
8 Orin S. Kerr, How to Read a Legal Opinion, 11 *Green Bag 2D* 51 (2007).
9 J. H. Baker, *Manual of Law French*, 194 (1979) ("the common connotation of tort as a wrong distinct from contract is rarely found before xvii cent.").

See also David Mellinkoff, *The Language of the Law*, 15 (1963) (for a list of French words in the common law system).

10 R. C. Van Caenegem, *The Birth of the English Common Law*, 4–6 (1973).

11 John Norton Pomeroy, *A Treatise on Equity Jurisprudence, as Administered in the United States of America*, Vol. 1, §§10–11 (4th ed., 1918). See also John Hudson, *The Formation of the English Common Law: Law and Society in England from the Norman Conquest to Magna Carta*, 24–51 (for a more comprehensive overview of the courts in England during this time-period).

12 William F. Walsh, Equity Prior to the Chancellor's Court, 17 *Geo. L. J.* 97, 98 (1929).

13 John Norton Pomeroy, *A Treatise on Equity Jurisprudence, as Administered in the United States of America*, Vol. 1, §§10–11 (4th ed., 1918).

14 Joseph Henry Beale, Introduction, iii–xix, xvii, *in Ranulph de Glanville, A Treatise on the Laws and Customs of the Kingdom of England (John Beames trans., 1900)*.

15 *Timeline of Magna Carta and Its Legacy*, https://www.bl.uk/magna-carta/articles/timeline-of-magna-carta

16 Joseph Henry Beale, Introduction, iii–xix, xvii, *in Ranulph de Glanville, A Treatise on the Laws and Customs of the Kingdom of England (John Beames trans., 1900)*.

17 History of the Judiciary, https://www.judiciary.uk/about-the-judiciary/history-of-the-judiciary/

18 *Id.*

19 John Norton Pomeroy, *A Treatise on Equity Jurisprudence, as Administered in the United States of America*, Vol. 1, §§12–34 (4th ed., 1918).

20 William F. Walsh, Equity Prior to the Chancellor's Court, 17 *Geo. L. J.* 97 (1929).

21 Barry R. Nager, The Jury That Tried William Penn, 50 *American Bar Association Journal* 168, 169–170 (1964).

22 Scott Torow, Best Trial; Order in the Court, *New York Times Magazine* (1999), https://www.nytimes.com/1999/04/18/magazine/best-trial-order-in-the-court.html

23 William Hepworth Dixon, *History of William Penn: Founder of Pennsylvania*, 91–115 (1872).

24 *Id* at 107.

25 Barry R. Nager, The Jury That Tried William Penn, 50 *American Bar Association Journal* 168, 170 (1964).

26 Stephen Landsman, A Brief Survey of the Development of the Adversary System, 44 Ohio State Law Journal 713, 730 (1983).

27 John Norton Pomeroy, A Treatise on Equity Jurisprudence, as Administered in the United States of America, Vol. 1, §§40–41 (4th ed., 1918).

28 Judicature Act of 1873, Encyclopaedia Britannica, https://www.britannica.com/event/Judicature-Act-of-1873

29 Thomas Hobbes, Leviathan (1651); John Locke, Two Treatises of Government (1689); John Locke, A Letter Concerning Toleration (1689).

30 English Bill of Rights, History.com (March 6, 2018) ("Many historians also believe that the ideas of English philosopher John Locke greatly influenced the content of the [English] Bill of Rights.").

31 See generally William A. Edmundson, An Introduction to Rights (2nd ed. 2012).

32 Roscoe Pound, The Spirit of the Common Law (1921). College of Law, Faculty Publications, 1–2, http://digitalcommons.unl.edu/lawfacpub/1

33 Janet Ainsworth, Legal Discourse and Legal Narratives, 2 Language and Law / Linguagem e Direito 1, 3 (2015)

>   The adversarial justice model has historically been the established system in both the United Kingdom, its birthplace, and in its colonies and former colonial possessions, including the United States and Canada in North America; India, Pakistan, Singapore, Malaysia, and Hong Kong in Asia; Australia and New Zealand in the South Pacific; and nations such as Nigeria, Uganda, Kenya, and Tanzania in Africa...

>   (However, it should be noted that "[m]ore and more countries that traditionally maintained inquisitorial systems have come to adopt in whole or in part many of the characteristics of adversarial systems").

34 Walter V. Schaefer, Is the Adversary System Working in Optimal Fashion? in Addresses Delivered at the National Conference on the Causes of Popular Dissatisfaction with the Administration of Justice, 70 F.R.D. 79, 160 (1976).

35 See generally Arthur Isak Applbaum, Ethics for Adversaries: The Morality of Roles in Public and Professional Life (1999).

36 Warren E. Burger, Agenda for 2000 A.D.-A Need for Systematic Anticipation, in Addresses Delivered at the National Conference on the Causes of Popular Dissatisfaction with the Administration of Justice, 70 F.R.D. 79, 92–96 (1976).

37 *Id.* at 95.

38 See Walter K. Olson, *The Litigation Explosion: What Happened When America Unleashed the Lawsuit* (1991).

39 Walter V. Schaefer, Is the Adversary System Working in Optimal Fashion? *in Addresses Delivered at the National Conference on the Causes of Popular Dissatisfaction with the Administration of Justice*, 70 F.R.D. 79, 170–71 (1976).

40 Ozan Varol, Let's Kill All the Lawyers, *The Huffington Post* (2017).

41 *Id.* See also Debbie Vogel, 'Kill the Lawyers,' A Line Misinterpreted, *The New York Times* (1990), https://www.nytimes.com/1990/06/17/nyregion/l-kill-the-lawyers-a-line-misinterpreted-599990.html

2

THE AMERICAN RULE AND ENTREPRENEURIAL LITIGATION

While the United States continued many traditions of the English common law, over time, U.S. law began to develop independently, albeit still often influenced by its English roots. Like a growing child, the U.S. system regularly sought to distinguish itself from its English parent by developing its own viewpoints and practices. One of the most significant and impactful rules adhered to in the United States, but not in England, is what is aptly called the "American Rule" for attorneys' fees. The American Rule holds that absent a law or contractual provision that says otherwise, both parties to a dispute must pay their own attorneys' fees. This rule is quite different than its English counterpart, sometimes called the "English Rule" or the "Loser-Pays Rule" which mandates that the losing party is required to pay (at least a portion of) the prevailing party's fees. The American Rule, in combination with other socio-economic factors (e.g., the contingency fee), has contributed to a rise in entrepreneurial litigation in the United States by incentivizing the filing of lawsuits.

DOI: 10.4324/9780429507847-4

Historical Development of the American Rule: Its Successes and Failures

The American Rule's general prescription that each party should pay their own fees has more exceptions than perhaps any other rule in U.S. law. The American Rule's exceptions are largely creatures of statutes, but these are not the only exceptions.[1] Legislative permissions, judicial views, and public endorsements of the American Rule and its exceptions have evolved over time.[2] In this evolutionary process, the American Rule has diverged significantly from its English counterpart and most of the rest of the world. The divergence arises primarily as a function of the different statutes promulgated in England and the United States to govern the awarding of attorneys' fees. England adopted a statutory Loser-Pays system, while the United States developed a more complex system composed of numerous exceptions to the American Rule, most arising via statute and procedural rules but some through equity and common law.

During the early days of colonial America, many colonial courts regulated attorney's fees by statute.[3] During at least the late colonial period, several courts fixed the amount the lawyer could receive from the client as the same as what the client could recover from the court.[4] That is, the lawyer was not allowed to charge the client more than the court could award in attorneys' fees. Some commentators suggest that attempts at regulating lawyer fees arose as a result of anti-lawyer hostility, yet others suggest it was merely a function of an economy that was regulated in a variety of areas including lawyer fees.[5]

By the end of the eighteenth century, the American Rule, as it is known today, was publicly pronounced. The U.S. Supreme Court enunciated in its early days that the awarding of attorneys' fees is in opposition to the "general practice of the United States ... and even if that practice were not strictly correct in principle, it is entitled to the respect of the court, till it is changed, or modified, by statute."[6] Indeed, even England's Loser-Pays system was a function of a statutory system that modified previous practices.[7] Large-scale attempts to convert to a Loser-Pays system in the United States have faced considerable political push-back,[8] although some states, most notably Alaska, have invoked Loser-Pays rules in at least some areas of practice. In other areas, the American Rule is revered, with one Circuit Court

Judge referring to it as "the hallowed American rule."[9] There is a juxtaposition of both reverence and criticism of the American Rule by American jurists.

Today, the most common judicial carve-outs to the American Rule include contracts, bad faith, the common fund doctrine, the substantial benefit rule, and contempt.[10] These common law carve-outs, however, vary by state and in some states have been supplanted by statute. There are thousands of statutory and procedural rule exceptions to the American Rule under federal and state laws.[11] Most, however, are one-way attorney fee-shifting statutes that "grant attorney fee recovery routinely to prevailing plaintiffs but rarely to prevailing defendants."[12] These one-way attorney fee-shifting statutes incentivize litigation in designated areas within which plaintiffs have little to lose and everything to gain by pursuing litigation. Such areas often include civil rights, environmental, employment law actions, and other areas that the plaintiff is often presumed to be in a weaker power-position to the defendant, or that social or policy considerations lead to a desire to increase the ease of access to the courts. One-way attorney fee-shifting statutes can enable access to justice for certain plaintiffs. They can simultaneously encourage vexatious litigation by, among others, disgruntled employees. The paragraphs that follow consider the pros and cons of the American Rule.

Arguments against the American Rule

When it comes to financial investing strategies, there are very few investments one can make that have low risk and large potential for gains. Investing in stocks is said to be a risky activity but could lead to significant monetary gains. Bonds are said to be low-risk investments, but bonds will not likely lead to significant monetary gains. Leave it to the U.S. court system to create a low-risk activity with the potential for large monetary gains. These investments are called lawsuits. For a minimal monetary investment (perhaps just costs) a plaintiff can hire an attorney on a contingency basis, pay no attorney's fees unless if the attorney wins, has no risk of paying the other party's fees, and maintains the potential for a large payout upon settlement of the case. The odds of winning a lawsuit are often better than playing the lottery or trying one's hand in Vegas so few, if given the opportunity, would choose not to sue under such favorable circumstances.

Lord Denning, a highly respected English judge, says this another way:

> As a moth is drawn to the light, so is a litigant drawn to the United States. If he can only get his case into their courts, he stands to win a fortune. At no cost to himself, and at no risk of having to pay anything to the other side. The lawyers there will conduct the case "on spec" as we say, or on a "contingency fee" as they say. The lawyers will charge the litigant nothing for their services but instead they will take 40% of the damages, if they win the case in court, or out of court on a settlement. If they lose, the litigant will have nothing to pay to the other side. The courts in the United States have no such costs deterrent as we have. There is also in the United States a right to trial by jury. These are prone to award fabulous damages. They are notoriously sympathetic and know that the lawyers will take their 40% before the plaintiff gets anything. All this means that the defendant can be readily forced into a settlement. The plaintiff holds all the cards.[13]

Denning's comments have been said to represent the English view of the American Rule and associated court practices.[14] One need not, however, cross the pond to find criticisms of the U.S. civil litigation system. There are many critics both within and outside the United States. As these arguments go, the American Rule and associated practices lead to an increase in frivolous claims and unnecessary congestion of the court system.[15]

The unfortunate consequence of these risk-takers initiating litigation is that the other party, the defendant, regardless of who wins or loses, must bear the considerable cost of defending a lawsuit. While contingency fee arrangements are common in many areas for plaintiff's work, they are rarely, if ever, available for a defendant. The defendant thus has the burden of bearing the costs of defending a lawsuit, even if meritorious. The costs of defending a lawsuit can be substantial and it is not uncommon that small businesses and individuals cannot afford the high cost of fees. This may lead to bankruptcies or businesses closing. The American Rule leads to an adversarial system that is stacked in favor of plaintiffs, particularly when one-way fee-shifting statutes are involved, and those plaintiffs literally have everything to gain and little to lose. However, if the plaintiff loses, the defendant is never "made whole." On the other hand, if there is no one-way fee-shifting statute available for a particular lawsuit (e.g., many tort claims), then the criticism is that neither party is "made whole" from the litigation.

Corresponding with these criticisms are the interrelated concerns that the American Rule does not effectively deter parties from running up exorbitant legal fees by, for instance, engaging in stalling tactics, filing unnecessary motions, or engaging in excessive discovery. Such tactics increase the legal costs and, as the argument goes, these tactics will decrease if losers of lawsuits are required to pay the fees of the winners.[16] This concern is particularly salient in areas of law that invoke one-way fee-shifting statutes. In these areas, plaintiffs may run up higher legal bills than necessary knowing full well that they may recover these attorneys' fees if they win, and that there is little to no chance that they will have to pay the other party's fees, even if they lose the case.

Another consequence of incentivizing the potential for large payouts is that legitimate cases with the potential for only small payouts are disfavored by many attorneys who would rather spend their time on bigger cases involving more money. This may prevent attorneys from getting involved in smaller cases and make it difficult for plaintiffs with legitimate claims of lesser value to gain access to justice.[17] While contingency fees may involve large fee awards, clients are regularly asked to cover the costs (e.g., filing fees, service fees, depositions, mailing fees) which can easily measure in the thousands of dollars even for small cases. This decreases the access to the courts for parties with claims of lesser value and for poorer parties that cannot afford to pay costs. It also incentivizes attorneys to focus their time and efforts on cases with larger payouts, so that they can recover a larger contingency fee.

A less obvious consequence of the American Rule regards the obstacle it has created for developing a harmonized system of international private law. The American Rule is largely foreign to much of the rest of the world. Few other countries utilize similar methods when it comes to fees.[18] Yet, absent a specifically carved-out exception for international private law, any such issues that are litigated in the United States are subject to the American Rule. This creates inequities for those enforcing international rights in the courts of the many nations. The inequitable result is apparent in the ongoing debate over whether attorneys' fees are recoverable under the United Nations Convention on Contracts for the International Sale of Goods (CISG) when CISG governed contracts are litigated in the United States.[19] This debate reveals the problems that can arise with international relations when the United States takes an approach so very different from the rest of the world.

Arguments for the American Rule

Despite its drawbacks, there are many proffered benefits of the American Rule when it comes to attorneys' fees. Ironically, some of the proffered benefits are similar to some of the criticisms. Some claim, for instance, that the American Rule does increase access to justice, as opposed to decrease it. As this argument goes, the American Rule allows honest people to bring lawsuits without the fear of having to pay the other party's fees if they lose. Having to bear the cost of claims could decrease the potential for litigation because parties will be deterred from bringing illegitimate claims. Initiating a Loser-Pays system could increase litigation. If proper caps on fees were not initiated along with it, there is a danger that attorneys will charge a higher fee than necessary knowing that they will be able to recover it. Such caps, however, could undermine free market principles and freedom of contract. Placing limits on the amount of the fee recoverable would need to be regulated. If attorneys could charge more than the permissible recoverable fee, then parties may still be required to carry substantial costs.

A touted benefit of the American Rule is that it is more favorable than the Loser-Pays Rule in promoting cases involving innovative claims and claims with costly defenses. Some cases require testing before they are successful, and such testing may not be available if plaintiffs are burdened with the fees of prevailing defendants. Such testing occurred with the asbestos litigations which required "costly failures that gradually unearthed the facts" prior to successes by plaintiffs.[20] Similarly, when a defendant's recoverable expenses are significantly greater than the plaintiff's expenses, the plaintiff in a Loser-Pays regime may be deterred from bringing suit for fear of paying those expenses. Under the American Rule, in many cases, such claims may be brought without fear of paying the legal fees of the defense.[21]

Another proffered advantage of the American Rule is that it limits court disputes over the amount of attorneys' fees.[22] That is, at least, when there are no one-way fee-shifting statutes or other mechanisms for recovering fees. When fee awards are authorized by contract, statute, or otherwise, there will inevitably be disputes over the amount of those fees. The American Rule does limit the volume of these disputes by limiting the circumstances that fees can be awarded. In some Loser-Pays jurisdictions, and particularly those jurisdictions with flexible or "reasonableness" standards associated with their fee awards, disputes do often arise, and add to the burden on the court system.[23]

Finally, the American Rule allows for one-way fee-shifting in statutorily authorized cases.[24] This allows for legislatures to create incentives for plaintiffs' attorneys in areas that the legislature would like to encourage litigation such as civil rights, environmental protection, and other worthwhile areas. The one-way fee-shifting is a mechanism that does motivate attorneys to bring claims in areas in need of societal repair.

The Many Types of Loser-Pays Systems

Although the American Rule is generally compared to the Loser-Pays Rule, the "American Rule" and "Loser-Pays Rule" descriptors may themselves be a false dichotomy that is "hopelessly simplistic as well as virtually useless."[25] There are many different systems that fall under the broad heading of "Loser-Pays" across many nations. It is not an all-or-nothing choice for legislatures who wish to impose some manner of fee payment on losing parties to lawsuits. Many countries place caps on the amount recoverable in the form of tariffs, percentages, or by utilizing a more flexible standard such as "reasonableness."[26] Even U.S. courts often allow for the prevailing party to recover some court costs from the losing party, but those costs, of course, typically do not include attorneys' fees. The variety of Loser-Pays regimes across the world results in generalizations about the benefits and downsides of Loser-Pays systems to be over simplified, because each unique Loser-Pays system arguably has some benefits and other downsides when compared to another.

The American Rule and Entrepreneurial Litigation

Attorneys should carefully evaluate each case. The probable amount of damages is a key factor in evaluating a case along with the veracity and likeability of the client, the supporting evidence, the merits, the time commitment, and the potential for a successful outcome. Whether or not there is an exception to the American Rule that allows for attorneys' fees to be recovered may be the determining factor in case selection. For instance, most U.S. states allow attorneys' fees to be recoverable if there is a contractual clause that authorizes fee recovery in a breach of contract action.

If there is no such clause in the contract, few U.S. states by statute or rule would allow for attorneys' fees to be recoverable for a breach of contract. Outside of those states, a contract without a fee-shifting clause could cost a plaintiff more to enforce than the plaintiff would be able to recover. Even a winning plaintiff could end up with a net loss when trying to enforce contractual rights.

Conversations with clients can be difficult. Having to tell a client "it may cost you more to enforce your rights in court than you will be able to recover" requires empathy and an explanation of other options. In response to such a statement, a client could react in a variety of ways. First, the client could assert that suing is a matter of principle and wants to sue regardless of the costs. Clients like this should be evaluated carefully to determine if their motivations are truly just or embedded in vengeance. Second, the client could concede that suing is just not worth the costs. Third, the client may want to know if there are other options. Fourth, the client may get angry and frustrated. How the client responds to this conversation should be viewed as a "clue" which may reveal what working with this client might be like. Other strategies, such as sending demand letters or mediation, should be discussed with the client, and considered in lieu of litigation, keeping in mind that the inability to recover attorneys' fees affects both parties to the contract. This equalization does create leverage for the plaintiff who has legitimate claims.

The conversation over the recoverability of attorneys' fees is intimately connected to the concept of the "private attorney general." The private attorney general is an attorney who is tasked with enforcing public rights, such as a plaintiff's attorney who brings Fair Labor Standards Act (FLSA) or environmental lawsuits. One common method of incentivizing private attorneys to enforce public rights is for legislatures to authorize fee awards for prevailing plaintiffs. John Coffee, a well-known critic of the private attorney general concept brutally criticizes the notion of the private attorney general, noting that the plaintiff's attorney "often looks less like a vigilant watchdog and more like a well-fed lapdog."[27] He further comments that the

> great vulnerability in the attorney general concept is then that the two active participants – defendant's and plaintiff's counsel – can collude to advance their interests to the detriment of those clients supposedly served. Often, this does not happen at first, but over time protocols develop, as both sides find that de facto collusion is the course of least resistance.[28]

The private attorney general concept, in other words, often leads to self-interest "triumphing over idealism."[29]

Coffee concludes that society must structure economic incentives in such a way as to motivate attorneys to fulfill desired social ends, while anticipating the self-interest motivated collusion, and deterring it to the extent possible.[30] Coffee further concludes that it "is unrealistic, even quixotic, to attempt to make the private attorney general truly virtuous, because it exists in a rough-and-tumble world."[31] While Coffee's observation that a "job that offers enormous returns to unscrupulousness will attract many unscrupulous persons and corrupt many persons of ordinary character,"[32] may lend itself to truth, this doesn't undercut the need to take steps to motivate lawyers toward ethical behaviors. Just as economic incentives can motivate lawyers toward certain types of cases, incentives can also be utilized to promote virtuous behavior in the legal field. For instance, judges are empowered to admonish (in written opinions) attorneys who skirt the line of ethical behaviors, thereby creating a record of those attorneys' unethical behavior. To incentivize virtue, judges could more regularly praise (in written opinions) attorneys who exhibit high standards of ethical excellence in a situation or case. Rewarding virtuous lawyers through such recognition would provide positive reinforcement for exemplary ethical performance before a judge.

Society has the responsibility to align economic incentives with virtuous behavior, and similarly to deter vice through not only judicial admonishments, but also through prudent legislation. The fault in Coffee's approach is that he does not sufficiently account for those plaintiff's attorneys who genuinely care and desire to serve the public good and the interests of their clients. Sometimes such interests are best achieved through what he calls "de facto collusion," because, by working with the opponent, the desired ends of a large settlement for the client become attainable. Simply because some are corrupted by the potential for enormous returns, doesn't necessitate that society should not strive to embed virtue into the nature of its citizens. Ethics education is perhaps the one recourse that could save a social and political system fraught with corruption from the ground to its highest tiers.

It is at this point that an important distinction should be made between ethics education, such as that taught in philosophy or business ethics classes, and the rules of professional conduct that are taught in law school professional responsibility classes. These rules later become the subject of Continuing Legal Education requirements that some refer to as "ethics requirements," in many states. Through ethics education that exceeds the professional rules in law schools, and aligning incentives with ethical outcomes, the legal industry could, over time, and person-by-person and decision-by-decision, improve in spirit and reputation.

Popular American culture acquiesces to the norms of litigiousness and accepts that some (perhaps whimsically) are waiting for their opportunity to sue to attain a large payout. However, the bad reputation of lawyers, and preconceptions of the "hired gun" model of attorney advocacy can be militated against over time. The current system which is said to benefit "lawyers unduly and the public inadequately"[33] requires a conscious rethinking from the foundation of education on up. Imagine a world wherein more embrace the maxim that lawyers are "admired more for their honesty (and/or humanity) than winning,"[34] a world where few lawyers would consider making payments to professional plaintiffs,[35] and a world where the profession of law is not overwhelmed by its business components.[36] This should be the world that law school education strives to create.

The next chapter, Chapter 3, moves beyond the American Rule and entrepreneurial litigation to analyze a variety of socio-economic factors that continue to impact the external environment of contemporary legal practice.

Notes

1 John Leubsdorf, Toward a History of the American Rule on Attorney Fee Recovery, 47 *Law and Contemporary Problems* 9, 9 (1984).

2 See generally *Id.*

3 *Id.* at 10–11.

4 *Id.* at 10 n. 8.

5 *Id.* at 11.

6 *Arcambel v. Wiseman*, 3 U.S. 306, 1 L. Ed. 613 (1796).

7 David A. Root, Attorney Fee-Shifting in America: Comparing, Contrasting, and Combining the "American Rule" and the "English Rule," 15 *Ind. Int'l & Comp. L. Rev.* 583, 590–591 (2005) (tracing the history and development of England's loser-pays system).

8 See generally Walter Olson and David Bernstein, Loser-Pays: Where Next? 55 *Maryland Law Review* 1161 (1996).

9   *Zapata Hermanos Sucesores, S.A. v. Hearthside Baking Co.*, 313 F.3d 385, 389 (7th Cir. 2002), *cert. denied*, 540 U.S. 1068 (2003).

10 John F. Vargo, The American Rule on Attorney Fee Allocation: The Injured Person's Access to Justice, 42 *Am. U.L. Rev.* 1567, 1578–1590 (1993).

11 *See also ATP Tour Inc. v. Deutscher Tennis Bund*, 91 A. 3d 554 (Del. 2014) (fee shifting in corporate bylaws permitted by Supreme Court of Delaware).

12 John Leubsdorf, Does the American Rule Provide Access to Justice? Is That Why It Was Adopted? 67 *Duke L.J. Online* 257, 258 (2019).

13 Smith Kline & French Laboratories Ltd. v. Bloch [1983], 2 *All ER* 72, 74 (C.A.).

14 W. Kent Davis, The International View of Attorney Fees in Civil Suits: Why Is the United States The "Odd Man Out" in How It Pays Its Lawyers? 16 *Ariz. J. Int'l & Comp. Law* 361 (1999).

15 John F. Vargo, The American Rule on Attorney Fee Allocation: The Injured Person's Access to Justice, 42 *Am. U.L. Rev.* 1567, 1591 (1993).

16 Walter Olson and David Bernstein, Loser-Pays: Where Next? 55 *Maryland Law Review* 1161, 1162 (1996).

17 John F. Vargo, The American Rule on Attorney Fee Allocation: The Injured Person's Access to Justice, 42 *Am. U.L. Rev.* 1567, 1591 (1993).

18 Japan and China, however, have systems more akin to the American Rule than the Loser-Pays Rule. See Craig I Celniker, Chie Yakura, Louise C Stoupe and Yuka Teraguchi, Litigation and Enforcement in Japan: Overview, *Thomson Reuters Westlaw Practical Law* (December 1, 2018), *global.practicallaw.com/ dispute-guide* (In Japan..."Each party must pay its own attorneys' fees, and the unsuccessful party is generally not liable to pay the successful party's attorneys' fees. However, if the successful party claims its attorneys' fees as part of its damages under contract, in tort or in a derivative suit, and the court orders the payment, as part of the judgment, the unsuccessful party must pay them. The court does not often order the payment of the attorneys' fees, and even when it does, the payment is normally limited to "reasonable" attorneys' fees, which usually covers only a part of the actual fees"); Zhang Shouzhi, Litigation and Enforcement in China: Overview, *Thomson Reuters Westlaw Practical Law* (June 1, 2017), *global.practicallaw. com/dispute-guide* (In China..."Usually, the parties pay their own attorney's fees. However, there are several occasions where the losing party may also be ordered to pay the winning party reasonable attorney's fees, such

as: Personal injury claims. Defamation claims. Infringement of copyright, trade mark or patent claims. Unfair competition. The court can award attorneys' fees, but will usually follow the recommended fee scale issued by the government. In large commercial disputes, the recoverable legal fees amount to a very small portion of actual expenses"); and Milena Dordevic, "Mexican Revolution" in CISG Jurisprudence and Case-Law: Attorneys' Fees as (Non)Recoverable Loss for Breach of Contract, *in Private Law Reform in South East Europe: Liber Amorcorum Christa Jessel-Holst*, 199, 202 n. 8 (Mirko S. Vasiljevic, Rainer Kulms, Tatjana Josipovic and Maja Stanivukovic eds., 2010).

19 See, for example, Bruno Zeller, Attorneys' Fees- Last Ditch Stand? 59 *Villanova L. R.* 761, 770 (2013); Bruno Zeller, *Damages Under the Convention on Contracts for the International Sale of Goods*, 139–160 (2nd ed., 2009); and Kathleen McGarvey Hidy and Keith William Diener, Damages Under CISG: Attorneys' Fees and Other Losses in International Commercial Law, 29 *Journal of Transnational Law and Policy* 1 (2019–2020).

20 John Leubsdorf, Does the American Rule Provide Access to Justice? Is That Why It Was Adopted? 67 *Duke L.J. Online* 257, 260 (2019).

21 *Id.*

22 *Id.* at 262–263.

23 *Id.* at 262–263.

24 *Id.* at 269–270.

25 See generally Mathias Reimann, *Cost and Fee Allocation in Civil Procedure: A Comparative Study*, 9 (2012) (discussing the variations among domestic methods of fee recovery and allocation in different countries).

26 *Id.* at 11.

27 John C. Coffee, Jr., *Entrepreneurial Litigation: Its Rise, Fall, and Future*, 44 (2015).

28 *Id.* at 50.

29 *Id.* at 152.

30 *Id.* at 235.

31 *Id.*

32 Walter K. Olson, *The Litigation Explosion: What Happened When America Unleashed the Lawsuit*, 33 (1991).

33 John C. Coffee, Jr., *Entrepreneurial Litigation: Its Rise, Fall, and Future*, 219 (2015).

34 James Gray Robinson, Top 10 Rules to Be a Successful Lawyer, *ABA Journal*, http://www.abajournal.com/voice/article/10-rules-for-being-a-successful-lawyer

35 John C. Coffee, Jr., *Entrepreneurial Litigation: Its Rise, Fall, and Future*, 76–77 (2015).

36 *Id.* at 234.

3

THE LAW SCHOOL AND LAWYER BOOM

The noble legal profession could once all but guarantee attorneys a comfortable and prosperous life. As the socio-economic climate shifted in the late twentieth and early twenty-first centuries, the profession began to evolve toward a business enterprise model. Many of the representatives of the people, the officers of the court, became savvy businesspeople who could not compete without the ability to market themselves and differentiate their talents above the rest to meet their "bottom-line" needs. Cronyism and connections began to pave the way to success as "who you know" became as important as "what you know."

There is no one event that can be recognized as causing the perceived downgrading of the value of the U.S. law degree, but rather there are many contributing factors including:

- The increase in the number of lawyers;
- The advent of new technologies;
- The decrease of trust in the legal profession;

DOI: 10.4324/9780429507847-5

- The increasing cost of becoming an attorney;
- A fluctuating economy;
- An increasing societal population; and
- Shifts in the political landscape.

The impact of these factors in the changing landscape of the legal field and the perceived devaluation of the law degree are discussed in this chapter. The central crux of the issue is that a law degree, while still valuable, is not quite worth what many people think. Simultaneously, there is evidence that despite these factors which contribute to the perceived downgrading of the law degree, the law degree remains a good investment for some.

The Increase in the Number of Lawyers

As more universities realized the profit potential of law schools, and began admitting students en masse, the principles of supply and demand took hold of the legal market. The legal profession became saturated with eager, newly minted attorneys looking for work. According to the American Bar Association (ABA), the number of registered lawyers in the United States has increased over 20-fold since 1880, with an approximate 15% increase from 2008 to 2018.[1] The number of law schools has risen to over 200 accredited schools which are rapidly churning out increasing numbers of lawyers.[2] The contemporary model of mass production of young attorneys has largely abandoned the apprenticeship model that preceded it.[3] Along with the increasing number of law schools and lawyers has come, for many in the field, a decrease in the average income.[4] Although many law schools are profit-centers for universities, some, such as the short-lived Indiana Tech Law School and Charlotte School of Law, have shuttered.[5] The great recession contributed to a decreasing morale among many in the legal field as news agencies reported lay-offs in prestigious law firms, and once power-house big firms went out of business. The media reported multiple suicides by laid-off attorneys.[6]

The so-called "American Dream" of going from rags to riches has come to fruition for some in the legal field. Perhaps because of the stories of the tobacco or asbestos litigation attorneys, or because of the occasionally reported over-sized attorneys' fee award,[7] or perhaps even because of advertised high hourly rates of attorneys, young money-eyed college graduates gravitate toward legal education in hopes of prosperity. Yet, the hourly rates are quickly off set by non-billable time, high overhead costs including, among many other costs: bar dues, continuing legal education (CLE) costs, malpractice insurance, office space, staff, benefits, and the technologies necessary to maintain an efficient practice. Some firms go unpaid by their clients and chase their clients down for unpaid fees, which, at times, leads to fee disputes or spitefully filed malpractice claims against the firms that are owed money by their clients.

The traditional wisdom that a law degree is a good investment has been challenged by many in recent times. As one commentator notes,

> [i]t may be that those who choose to pursue law degrees suffer from what one might label "career delusions": they know that a significant number of law graduates encounter trouble in launching a professional career, but they believe they are different.[8]

Regardless of these observations, there are still those who are willing to bear the opportunity costs and risks associated with going to law school.[9]

Commentators have noted the harsh realities of the legal market for aspiring attorneys, and particularly the market realities spurring from the 2008 recession.[10] One author commented that "[t]he Great Recession in 2008 has, for the first time, made prospective students wary of the notion that law school, however expensive, was an investment worth making."[11] Another author commented that "[i]n the future, most legal work will be cheaper, some work will be more expensive and most lawyers will be poorer."[12] Commentators have also noted that post-2008, many law school graduates failed to launch; as one author commented in 2010:

> Unemployment among new law school grads nationwide has risen for two straight years, to a rate of 12 percent for the class of 2009, according to the National Association for Law Placement. Among the employed, one in four jobs were temporary, while one in 10 were part-time. One-fifth of those employed said they were searching for another job, twice as many as in the boom years a decade ago. Recognizing the mounting crisis, the American Bar Association recently urged prospective students to carefully weigh the costs and benefits of a legal education. For a law degree to pay off, the association said in a memo, a grad should earn at least $65,000 a year. Nearly half of employed 2008 grads had starting salaries below that amount.[13]

The 2008 recession did lead to a dip in law school applications, and many queries about the value of a law degree. Despite the startling statistics, and the principles of supply and demand working against increasing income for lawyers, commentators rightly note that so long as law schools remain profit-centers, "the lawyer production machine will continue to churn out more lawyers,"[14] despite that "lawyers often do not earn enough income to pay off the debt incurred during law school."[15] The sad realities of capitalistic society intrude into legal academia, the legal field, and the many debt-ridden graduates entering the profession. The harsh realities of the legal market in the twenty-first century have also been impacted by the increasing utilization and efficiency of technology.

The Advent of New Technologies

The coronavirus pandemic of 2020 led to a shift in the way lawyers do business and courts hear cases. By necessity, the virtual tools that were available for years were implemented on a wide scale for client meetings, depositions, court hearings, and many other facets of the practice of law. Legal practice shifted to the cloud and online court filing became more accessible in courts that had not previously offered it. As governors, states, and the federal government attempted to manage the crisis, business went on for many attorneys, but with a new emphasis and need to adjust to and embrace new technologies.

Even prior to the pandemic, lawyers in the preceding decades had to adjust their practices to embrace new technologies, some of which had a direct impact on the legal market. The digital cataloguing of legal cases allowed lawyers to research and find relevant cases from a computer, instead of digging through stacks of books in law libraries or ordering expensive bounded case reporters. The move to digital communications and record keeping (such as email) in most businesses also changed the way that large-scale discovery was conducted, created a new competitive model, led to new businesses being founded to manage e-discovery, and new staffing agencies that provided temporary attorneys to work on large-scale document reviews. Some law firms moved to outsourcing tasks like document review to local temporary attorneys or to workers in other countries to reduce costs to clients.[16] In more recent times, predictive coding was marketed by some e-discovery vendors which, if utilized, would not require a human to even look at certain documents which may contain relevant information but instead decisions about a document's relevancy would be made based on patterns identified by computer programs. These new technologies and businesses decrease the need for law firms to maintain staff attorneys to handle tasks like document review, and instead temporary contractors are regularly hired to handle matters that were historically handled by law firm staff.

The blossoming of the internet provided the general public with a variety of new ways to gain access to legal documents and advice. Several companies entered the market selling fillable contracts, wills, powers of attorneys, and a variety of other legal documents that attorneys would have previously been hired to draft.[17] These documents are offered at low costs online, making it difficult for small firms to compete with the price-point, but having to market instead based on the individual attention and personalized tailoring of documents that attorneys can provide. Form documents are not always one-size-fits-all, but these online vendors often employ attorneys to ensure their products are cutting edge. These online vendors drive the market price down in certain areas of law. On the other hand, some specializations in law are inherently difficult to duplicate through technology or mass production; these fields may maintain the ability to charge high hourly rates in their niche practices despite technological evolution. Technology itself is not always trusted and must meet rigorous criteria if one desires to utilize technology as evidence in a court of law. Trust, however, poses an even broader dilemma for the legal profession.

The Decrease of Trust in the Legal Profession

Lawyers are not trusted.[18] According to one study, lawyers are included among the low-warmth, envied professions that engender respect but not trust.[19] A "warm" categorization involves perceptions that one is a friend as opposed to a foe, and is friendly and trustworthy.[20] Lawyers are perceived to be low in this "warmth" category and are often envied and resented, but simultaneously admired.[21] Common sense dictates that the lack of trust in lawyers contributes to the devaluing of the law degree to the extent that the lack of trust contributes to the decreased utilization of attorneys. Perhaps distrust or the associated envy and resentment contribute to fee disputes and downwardly negotiated payments. Decreasing trust in the legal profession is a major concern not only for the value of legal education but also for ensuring that perceived justice is the foundation of our system of government. As quite eloquently stated:

> It is every bit as urgent to preserve the minimum of trust that is the prime constituent of the social atmosphere in which all human interaction takes place. To be sure, a measure of caution and distrust is indispensable in most human interaction. Pure trust is no more conducive to survival in the social environment than is pure oxygen in the earth's atmosphere. But too high a level of distrust stifles efforts at cooperation as much as severe pollution impairs health.[22]

While deceit and secrecy by attorneys play a role in decreasing public trust in the legal field, attorneys themselves can be victims of lies, secrecy, and deceit as well. When clients fail to disclose information to their advocates, it can lead to disastrous results both for the client and for the representing attorneys. It can also result in the perception that the attorneys are to blame for the failure in the seeking of truth.

The importance of trust in the legal profession, and in one's own advocate is paramount. The level of trust directly impacts the involvement of individuals in relationships or organizations. People tend to lower their involvement when there is less trust and increase it when there is more trust.[23] Jaffe identifies six qualities that affect the degree of trust in another: (i) reliability and dependability; (ii) transparency; (iii) competency; (iv) sincerity, authenticity, and congruency; (v) fairness; and (vi) openness and vulnerability.[24] While most legal professionals seem to be reliable and dependable insofar as they can meet deadlines, the other qualities do vary significantly among the members of the legal profession. It may be that the lack of perceived sincerity and authenticity coupled with perceptions of unfairness in the legal system contribute to the distrust of lawyers. These qualities, however, can be improved by individual attorneys, which will, in turn, lead to an increase in trust. Such individual increases in trust are imperative considering that "trust is an ongoing exchange between people and is not static. Trust can be earned. It can be lost. And it can be regained."[25] Regaining trust tends to be a more difficult proposition than earning it, putting the legal profession in an uphill battle to regain the trust of its constituents.

Just as when trust is lost in a personal relationship, it is difficult to rebuild, and only with time and effort can one come to trust another who has, in the past, been untrustworthy. The more severe the violation of trust, the harder it typically is to rebuild. Lying to one's boss to take a sick day, while not a moral ideal, is a much easier breach of trust to rebuild particularly given the relative minor impact on others and proliferate use of the excuse in contemporary business. On the other hand, cheating on one's spouse proves a much more difficult breach of trust to rebuild given the intimacy of the relationship, the severe consequences, and the purported lifetime commitment. The legal field's breaches of trust have been relatively severe and repeated; as discussed in detail in Chapter 5, rebuilding that trust will be challenging because the field is composed of individuals many of whom have no concern for building trust with society, and only act out of concern for their personal interests.

It is nevertheless imperative to acknowledge that the legal profession is not the only industry suffering from distrust. It has been posited that "[p]eople today have 'trust issues' regarding all major institutions ... recent studies show that overall trust in government, media, business and other organizations is at an all-time low."[26] As population expands and personal relationships erode, society as a whole is losing trust in many of its institutions. Distrust of lawyers may be a symptom of a much larger disease that plagues contemporary society, perhaps because those who trust are often harmed and taken advantage of by the untrustworthy, and the untrustworthy themselves tend not to trust others. Lawyers themselves often adhere to the mantra of "trust but verify" or even, in more extreme cases, "don't trust and don't trust the verification." The need to win cases often outweighs other ethical considerations for at least some attorneys, and part of this perceived need arises because attorneys are saddled with high overhead costs.

The Increasing Cost of Becoming an Attorney

Everything comes with pain, but becoming an attorney is a particularly tumultuous pathway with a high price tag of admission. While averages and numerical figures change daily, what can be said is that the cost of a legal education has increased substantially compared to a generation ago.[27] Beyond tuition, books, and living expenses, there are a variety of hidden costs associated with law school education, including preparing for the Law School Admissions Test, law school preparatory classes, commercial outlines, and bar exam preparatory classes. These costs do not end with one being minted a licensed attorney, but rather increase as time goes on with malpractice premiums rising, bar dues ever increasing, and other expenses associated with the legal practice also leading to high overhead costs. These overhead costs can justify charging high billable hourly rates, but as is often the case, attorneys go beyond high hourly fees to finding creative ways to bill hours. A case that could be handled for a reasonable fee with a deep-pocketed client could easily lead to a windfall for the representing attorneys if they engage in vigorous motions practice, detailed and lengthy discovery, and drag out the proceedings to increase their billable hours. Such tactics represent the worst of the worst for the business of law, although many involved in the practice become numb to such concerns and acquiesce to the machinery of the billable hour.

Students graduating with large amount of debt, and student loan payments coming due, are often forced into volatile positions in law firms with survival of the fittest mentalities and, like a pack of wild dogs fighting over a meal, the attorneys compete for economic gain at the expense of and without hesitation for hurting others, even within their own firm. The more experienced attorneys put the new associates to work, often forcing long hours with minimal remuneration. The associates persevere with the glimmer of hope that once they gain the necessary experience that their lives will improve and that pot of gold at the end of the rainbow will be theirs. The alternatives to taking a job in a volatile environment, for some, only include taking on temporary positions, remaining unemployed, hoping something better comes along, or leaving the legal field altogether.

Over time, resentment often builds for the many attorneys who were not predestined to start their careers making large salaries at big firms. The delusions of riches that led many eager students to enter law school were, for some, enhanced by alleged inflated employment statistics of many law schools. After the glut of unemployed attorneys failed to enter the workforce following the great recession, many unemployed and underemployed law graduates opted to sue their law schools for inflating their advertised employment statistics.[28] While the economy was a major force in these graduates not finding jobs, it was perhaps not the sole cause of attorney unemployment. While after some time, most individuals who stick it out after law school achieve a reasonable income, it often comes at the expense of their mental or physical health deteriorating, personal or family relationships falling apart, or even struggles with addiction.[29] The pressures and competition increase when the economy takes a downturn.

A Fluctuating Economy

The ebbs and flows of the economy directly impact the viability of a successful career.[30] Research suggests that there are long-term negative economic effects to graduating in a year of a bad economy.[31] The contrary would seem to also hold true, that is, graduating in a year of a booming economy could have long-term positive economic effects on the graduating students. The generation that graduated law school in the early millennium faced not only the great recession of 2008 but also the coronavirus pandemic of 2020. It was reported in June 2020, amidst the pandemic, that almost half of the U.S. working age population did not have jobs.[32]

The pandemic led to law firm lay-offs, cancellations or postponements of summer associate programs, furloughs, pay reductions, voluntary buyouts, delays in the offering of bar examinations, and (at least for a time) a reduction in the utilization of legal services.[33] For recent law school graduates, the pandemic led to job offers being rescinded, primarily in private practice areas.[34] The reduction and delay in law jobs resulted in a market with an oversupply of eager attorneys all fighting for the same positions. Keeping those highly coveted positions, once attained, increases the pressure on attorneys and, at times, does contribute to ethical lapses.

As many law students graduating in 2020 had virtual graduation celebrations, delayed or online bar examinations, and delayed or rescinded job offers, the great recession of 2008 came to mind for many who had lived through similar occurrences only a decade prior.[35] Almost 53,000 net jobs were lost in the legal sector between March and July 2020, leading to a difficult market for the 2020 law graduates.[36] The market is directly impacted by the increase in societal population.

An Increasing Societal Population

The U.S. and world population are growing so quickly that the job market, even when growing, is not always able to keep up.[37] The rapid pace of population growth in the United States alone currently results in an estimated net gain of more than one person per minute in the United States.[38]

Resources are required to manage the increasing population, but resources are limited. The masses are left to battle for the limited resources including spots in law schools, law firms, government, and other industries. On the other hand, a larger population means a greater need for services.[39] As populations rise, so does competition in the marketplace, and so long as there is no short supply of lawyers to handle the rising population, one can only conjecture that the resources will continue to spread disproportionately thinner.

The impact of a growing societal population and the depletion of resources has an impact on all industries and as other industries and government grow to manage the population, the legal industry may have the opportunity to grow alongside them. Political changes present an opportunity to increase employment for legal professionals in certain areas where societal needs and policies may influence the desire for growth or enforcement in certain areas of law.

Shifts in the Political Landscape

Changing political landscapes lead to changing legal infrastructures, and, in turn, impact the need for lawyers in specialty fields. One new statute could create a new niche practice area for lawyers who engage it. An executive order implementing a new policy could change the way that cases in a certain field are handled and impact the likelihood of success for those engaged in the impacted practice area. Political changes carry with them changes to policy, laws, the composition of judges sitting on courts, how laws are interpreted and enforced, available resources for government legal jobs, and a variety of other facets of the legal profession. The New Deal spurred a need for social security lawyers. The Civil Rights Act of 1964 spurred the need for employment discrimination lawyers. New legislation inevitably spurs lawyers who learn the nuances of that legislation and practice to enforce the rights, duties, or restrictions under the legislation.

The law as the traditional gateway to politics further magnifies the inextricable relationship between a changing political landscape and changes to the legal field.[40] Many U.S. presidents have been trained in the law, and initiate reforms to the law. Bill Clinton successfully passed the Family Medical Leave Act after the Bush administration failed to pass similar legislation allowing for leave for eligible employees for family and medical issues, such as the birth of a child.[41] Barrack Obama passed the Affordable Care Act which, at the time, required everyone to have health insurance or pay a tax for not having it.[42] This individual mandate, however, was dismantled by Donald Trump's tax reforms, but pieces of Obama's legislation, including the employer mandate remained longer in effect. Both Clinton and Obama were trained at prestigious law schools, and their legislative initiatives resulted in a variety of lawsuits some arising to enforce the rights granted by the legislation and some, as in the case of the Affordable Care Act, to challenge the constitutionality of the act itself.[43]

The Value of the Law Degree

The increase in the number of lawyers, the advent of new technologies, the decrease of trust in the legal profession, the increasing cost of becoming an attorney, a fluctuating economy, an increasing societal population, shifts in the political landscape, and other socio-economic factors have combined to create the perception that graduating lawyers are in less prosperous circumstances than prior generations. Yet, despite these many factors, there is evidence that many who pursue a law degree, and particularly those who do so early in life, are financially better off, over the lifetime of their careers than those with only a bachelor's degree.[44] There is also evidence that opportunities are increasing for those with law degrees in other areas that diverge in whole or part from the traditional practice of law.[45] While some signals are positive, the changing socio-economic climate of the profession and the perceived devaluation of the law degree does contribute to some lawyers engaging in questionable ethical practices.

While socio-economic factors surely impact ethical behavior in the legal field, as discussed in greater detail in Chapter 9, lawyers should caution against normalizing and justifying unethical behavior based on rationalizations such as financial considerations. The next chapter, Chapter 4, introduces the *Giving Voice to Values* methodology, and explains how it can be used by legal practitioners to develop strategies for acting on their values.

Notes

1 ABA National Lawyer Population Survey, https://www.americanbar. org/content/dam/aba/administrative/market_research/Total%20

National%20Lawyer%20Population%201878-2017.authcheckdam.pdf; and New ABA Data Reveals Rise is the Number of U.S. Lawyers 15 Percent Increase since 2008 (May 11, 2018), https://www.americanbar.org/news/abanews/aba-news-archives/2018/05/new_aba_data_reveals/

2   ABA-Approved Law Schools, https://www.americanbar.org/groups/legal_education/resources/aba_approved_law_schools/

3   Mark T. Flahive, The Origins of the American Law School, 64 *American Bar Association Journal* 1868 (December 1978).

4   Benjamin H. Barton, The Fall and Rise of Lawyers, *CNN* (May 23, 2015), https://www.cnn.com/2015/05/22/opinions/barton-rise-and-fall-of-lawyers/

5   Elizabeth Olson, For-Profit Charlotte School of Law Closes, *NY Times* (August 15, 2017), https://www.nytimes.com/2017/08/15/business/dealbook/for-profit-charlotte-school-of-law-closes.html; and Marilyn Odendahl, Indiana Tech's Closing of Law School Leaves Unanswered Questions, *The Indiana Lawyer* (May 26, 2017), https://www.theindianalawyer.com/articles/43828-indiana-techs-closing-of-law-school-leaves-unanswered-questions

6   Richard B. Schmitt, A Death in the Office, *ABA Journal* (November 2, 2019), https://www.abajournal.com/magazine/article/a_death_in_the_office; See also Richard W. Bourne, The Coming Crash in Legal Education: How We Got Here and Where We Go Now, 45 *Creighton L. R.* 651, 651 (2012).

7   Keith William Diener, A Battle for Reason: The Unconscionable Attorney-Client Fee Agreement, 2016 *J. of the Prof. Lawyer* 129 (2016).

8   Herbert M. Kritzer, Law Schools and the Continuing Growth of the Legal Profession, 3 *Onati Socio-Legal Series* 450, 468 (2013).

9   Opportunity costs associated with going to law school may include (but are not limited to): three years of lost income from not working full-time while in law school, the accumulation of student loans with compounding interest rates, the delay of investments and other life opportunities (such as buying a home), and the reality that three years of one's life will be buried in case books - essentially committing those who enter law school straight from undergraduate to lose the prime years of their youth. Those that make the sacrifice early have more time to instrumentalize the law degree and to potentially attain a return on their law school investment.

10   *Fordham Law Review* published a symposium edition dedicated to changes to the legal industry spurring from the great recession, see Eli Wald, Forward: The Great Recession and the Legal Profession, 17 *Fordham Law Review* 2051 (2010).

11 Richard W. Bourne, The Coming Crash in Legal Education: How We Got Here and Where We Go Now, 45 *Creighton L. R.* 651, 678 (2012).

12 Benjamin H. Barton, A Glass Half Full Look at the Changes in the American Legal Market, 38 *International Review of Law and Economics* 29, 31 (2014).

13 Leslie Kwoh, *Irate Law School Grads Say They Were Misled About Job Prospects*, NJ (Updated Jan 18, 2019; Posted Aug 15, 2010), https://www.nj.com/business/2010/08/irate_law_school_grads_say_the.html; See also Noam Scheiber, An Expensive Law Degree and No Place to Use It, *The New York Times* (June 17, 2016), https://www.nytimes.com/2016/06/19/business/dealbook/an-expensive-law-degree-and-no-place-to-use-it.html

14 William D. Henderson and Rachel M. Zahorsky, The Law School Bubble: How Long Will It Last if Law Grads Can't Pay Bills? *ABA Journal* (January 1, 2012), https://www.abajournal.com/magazine/article/the_law_school_bubble_how_long_will_it_last_if_law_grads_cant_pay_bills

15 Richard W. Bourne, The Coming Crash in Legal Education: How We Got Here and Where We Go Now, 45 *Creighton L. R.* 651, 674 (2012).

16 See generally William D. Henderson, From Big Law to Lean Law, 38 *International Review of Law and Economics* 5 (2014).

17 See generally Benjamin H. Barton, A Glass Half Full Look at the Changes in the American Legal Market, 38 *International Review of Law and Economics* 29 (2014).

18 Susan T. Fiske and Cydney Dupree, Gaining Trust as Well as Respect in Communicating to Motivated Audiences About Science Topics, 111 *Psychology and Public Affairs* 13593, 13595 (2014), https://www.pnas.org/content/pnas/111/Supplement_4/13593.full.pdf

19 *Id.*

20 *Id.* at 13594.

21 *Id.*

22 Sissela Bok, Can Lawyers Be Trusted, 138 *University of Pennsylvania Law Rev.* 913, 920 (1990).

23 Dennis Jaffe, The Essential Importance of Trust: How to Build it or Restore It, *Forbes* (December 5, 2018), https://www.forbes.com/sites/dennisjaffe/2018/12/05/the-essential-importance-of-trust-how-to-build-it-or-restore-it/#5d6b65af64fe

24 *Id.*

25 *Id.*

26 Shawn Porat, Why Trust is a Critical Success Factor for Business Today, *Forbes* (July 7, 2017), https://www.forbes.com/sites/theyec/2017/07/07/why-trust-is-a-critical-success-factor-for-businesses-today/#44ccbb545dfo

27 See generally Richard W. Bourne, The Coming Crash in Legal Education: How We Got Here and Where We Go Now, 45 *Creighton L. R.* 651 (2012); William D. Henderson and Rachel M. Zahorsky, The Law School Bubble: How Long Will It Last If Law Grads Can't Pay Bills? *ABA Journal* (January 1, 2012), Brian Z. Tamanaha, How to Make Law School Affordable, *New York Times* (May 31, 2012).

28 See, e.g., Joe Palazolo, A Dozen Law Schools Hit with Lawsuits over Jobs Data, *The Wall Street Journal* (February 1, 2012).

29 Aileen Reilly, Are Attorneys and Marriage Compatible, *Law Practice Today* (August 15, 2018), https://www.lawpracticetoday.org/article/attorneys-marriage-compatible/

30 Janet Adamy, Millennials Slammed By Second Financial Crisis Fall Even Further Behind, *The Wall Street Journal* (August 9, 2020).

31 *Id.*

32 Yun Li, Nearly Half the U.S. Population is Without a Job, Showing How Far the Labor Recovery Has to Go, *CNBC* (June 30, 2020), https://www.cnbc.com/2020/06/29/nearly-half-the-us-population-is-without-a-job-showing-how-far-the-labor-recovery-has-to-go.html

33 Legal Executive Institute, Law Firm Updates: COVID-19's Impact on the Business of Law, *Thomson Reuters* (July 20, 2020), https://www.legalexecutiveinstitute.com/law-firm-updates-covid-19/; See also Anna-Maria Andriotis, No Jobs, Loads of Debt: Covid Upends Middle-Class Family Finances, *The Wall Street Journal* (September 20, 2020).

34 Elizabeth Olson, Pandemic Clobbers Job Starts for Law Graduates, *Bloomberg Law* (July 15, 2020) ("Nearly half of the 167 schools participating in the National Association for Law Placement survey reported that graduates had employment offers rescinded and 85% of schools said most involved private practice.")

35 Meghan Tribe, Bob Van Voris, and Stephanie Russel-Kraft, The Pandemic is Putting Law Students' Futures On Hold, *Bloomberg Businessweek* (April 14, 2020); see also Law School Grads Hit 12-Year Employment High Before Pandemic, *Bloomberg Law* (August 12, 2020), https://news.bloomberglaw.com/us-law-week/law-school-grads-hit-12-year-employment-high-before-pandemic-1

36 Caroline Spiezio, Pandemic Poised to Wipe Out Recession Rebound in Law Grad Hiring, Associate Pay, *Westlaw Today* (August 12, 2020).

37 Wolf Richter, The Job Market Isn't Getting Any Better, *Business Insider* (August 8, 2016).

38 U.S. and World Population Clock, United States Census Bureau, https://www.census.gov/popclock/ (As of October 2020, estimating one birth every 8 seconds, one death every 12 seconds, one net international migrant every 47 seconds, and thus a net gain of one person every 18 seconds).

39 Alan Sweezy and Aaron Owens, The Impact on Population Growth on Employment, 64 *American Economic Review* 45 (May 1974).

40 Walter Olson, *Schools for Misrule: Legal Academia and an Overlawyered America*, 1–3 (2011).

41 Keith William Diener, The Broadening Scope of the FMLA Compliance Period: Employers, Yield and Proceed with Caution! 15 *Atl. L. J.* 96 (2013).

42 Keith William Diener, The Ethics of Healthcare Reform: Coordinating Rights with Commoditization, *in Managing Integrated Health Systems* (John Shiver and John Cantiello eds., Jones & Bartlett Publishers 2015).

43 Walter Olson, *Schools for Misrule: Legal Academia and an Overlawyered America*, 1–3 (2011).

44 Michael Simkovic and Frank McIntyre, The Economic Value of a Law Degree, 43 *The Journal of Legal Studies* 249 (2014).

45 See, e.g., Jennifer Pacella, The Regulation of Lawyers in Compliance, 95 *Washington Law Review* 947 (2020).

Part II

THE ATTORNEY AS ADVOCATE

Part II turns to the individual legal practitioner who works in the contemporary legal environment. It examines the role of the attorney as an advocate and the core values of advocacy. These values are defined and explored in the context of the adversarial setting of the practice of law. The strategies of *Giving Voice to Values* are examined and implemented to decipher ways of expressing values effectively in legal contexts. This Part then turns to the attorney's challenge of building trust with stakeholders and adapts Tim Fort's tripartite vision of trust to the practice of law. Developing trust with clients and other stakeholders is a key component of effective advocacy. Following the examination of trust, this Part investigates the unethical employer and firm environment. It provides an outline of a process for subordinates who desire to address unethical and unprofessional conduct of their superiors in firm settings, while giving due consideration to legal and ethical concerns. Part II is aimed at examining the attorney's role as an advocate and how that role can be enhanced by adherence to values.

DOI: 10.4324/9780429507847-6

4

VOICING VALUES IN AN ADVERSARIAL ENVIRONMENT

Giving Voice to Values (GVV) provides a heuristic for implementing values in organizational settings.[1] GVV builds on the notion that we all have values and most people typically want to act in accordance with them. Advocacy presents unique values questions often resulting from conflicts between one's personal values and the values of a client or others within the profession. Regardless of how these interests diverge there is a set of core values that all advocates should share including zealousness, respect, responsibility, integrity, and honesty. Implementing these values in adversarial settings can be done, but it requires preparing oneself for the hell that sometimes is other people and recognizing that while the normative ideal is that advocates share these values, one must be prepared for the non-ideal world and the unfortunate reality that all do not.

Advocacy in the Adversarial Environment

While technologies can duplicate transactional aspects of the law, they are incapable of replacing a skilled advocate who is trained at making legal

DOI: 10.4324/9780429507847-7

arguments and inspiring others to their viewpoint. As one commentator expresses, "[w]hen we wonder what makes a great lawyer better than an average lawyer, very often the answer is found in what we call advocacy."[2] Advocates effectively represent client interests, speak on behalf of a client, and convince others why a client should prevail under the law. Advocates typically strive to make the best argument they can under the law given the unique facts of each case. While advocacy is often associated with the court-room, with terms such as "trial advocacy," it is not limited to courtroom contexts, but extends to every interaction the lawyer, as an agent, makes on behalf of a client. The interactions with judges, opposing counsels, wit-nesses, vendors, and every other human interaction on behalf of a client present opportunities for effective advocacy.

Many aspects of a case rely on effective advocacy. As one commentator explains, "the legal system relies heavily on advocacy by counsel of his cli-ent's objectives to achieve its most important goals."[3] Cases can be won or lost because of the skills an advocate maintains in balancing respect for the court, and zealous representation. This balancing act, like an Aristotelian moral virtue, often exists in the mean between two extremes – finding the appropriate middle way to effectively say what needs to be said while respecting the orders and inquiries of a judge and the inevitable interrup-tions of the opposition. Overzealous attorneys may try to present their pre-scripted arguments to a judge when a judge has already read the motions papers, and just wants clarification on a few items. Experienced advocates learn that sometimes not arguing and just answering the judge's questions is the best way to advocate for a client. Advocacy is more of an art than a science and involves the voicing of values on behalf of others.

Overview of Giving Voice to Values (GVV)

The GVV initiative was birthed by Dr. Mary Gentile. It is an action-oriented approach to implementing values judgments in a variety of organizational settings. GVV began as a method for teaching ethics in business by examining ways to implement our values after we've made the decision about what is right or wrong. While originating as a tool for teaching, GVV provides many insights that could be utilized in various industries, including the legal field. Among other values conflicts, GVV provides advocates with a methodology for preparing for the inevitable conflicts between zealous representation and respect to court and opposing counsel. Within the GVV framework lies the assumption that "we are more likely to find the courage and commitment to act on our values if we can find the words to express them persuasively, to ourselves and to others."[4] This assumption rings true in advocacy contexts where the power of the word plays so significant a role in attaining results for clients. Advocacy involves being able to listen and respond effectively and efficiently, while maintaining a sense of calm when utilizing facts and law to powerfully persuade. The pre-scripting techniques of GVV can prepare one for the various situations one will encounter in litigation, by examining hypotheticals and analyzing them according to the GVV methodology.

Carolyn Plump applies the GVV framework to various real-life situations from her years of experience in the legal profession.[5] She frames her ethical inquiry around three primary questions: (i) "What is at stake for the key parties"? (ii) "What arguments or rationalizations will the person wishing to voice his or her values likely encounter"? (iii) "What strategies can the person wishing to voice his or her values use to counter these arguments and plot a course of action"?[6] The examination of these questions provides a foundation for how GVV may be utilized by advocates, in a way that goes well beyond compliance with professional rules.

Robert Feldman also attempts to move beyond compliance with the rules. He emphasizes the balance among (i) the business of law, (ii) compliance with professional rules, and (iii) achieving one's values.[7] There is much more to engaging ethically with the legal profession and those within it than the compliance approach utilized by many law school professional responsibility classes and legal ethics CLEs. While professional rules are a starting point for inquiry, the inquiry should not stop there: the conversation needs to be changed from "can we do this?" to "should we do this?" and the answer to the latter question should not depend on bottom-line results. Once the "should" question is answered, the GVV precepts take hold and the question becomes "how can we do this?" given internal and external factors including the social, political, and economic environment.

The GVV approach is about deciphering strategies for implementing values once one has decided the right thing to do. Such strategies are inevitably fact-specific, and what may work in one set of circumstance would not work in a slightly different scenario. While pre-scripting is a helpful tool, one must be cautious not to rely on pre-scripted responses when addressing real-life situations because the stakeholders, events, and circumstances will inevitably vary from the hypotheticals. While good tools for learning, advocates who wish to voice values must move beyond pre-scripted responses and flow with the movements of the court and opposing counsel to effectively advocate values on behalf of another. This is much easier expressed in theory than performed in practice, or, to put it in common parlances, successfully flowing with the movements of court and opposing counsel is much "easier said than done." Indeed, GVV is a living approach that flows with the movements and responses of those involved.

While one may determine, for example, that mediation is the right approach to a given legal dispute, deciphering strategies to get the other side to come to the table and engage in mediation is another issue entirely. What is best for one's clients is not always best for the opposition, yet there are benefits to guided resolutions for everyone, including the peace of mind that comes from the finalization of a dispute without the psychologically exhausting experience of litigation. The scripted benefits of mediation also include the ability to tailor your own solution to your disagreement, reduced costs, a faster process, and a more confidential means of resolving disputes. Most attorneys learn these purported benefits of mediation in law school so repeating them to the opposition is fruitless, if not naïve. Other approaches to get an opposing party to come to the mediation table should be considered within the context of each dispute. When the dispute is of public interest, for example, one such tactic is involving the media. Media involvement can create a positive image for a client and pressure the other party to come to the table and mediate. However, it is important to ensure that the client and attorney are on the same page when it comes to strategic decisions such as media involvement.

A client's directives may sometimes conflict with what an attorney believes is the right thing to do. Consider how Jenny, a junior attorney, handled this values conflict in the following example.

THE LITIGIOUS CLIENT[8]

Jenny was a junior attorney who was assigned by her senior partner to represent Sam, a very litigious client, in a lawsuit. Sam was "out for blood" and wanted to do everything possible to make the opposing party in the lawsuit ("Jim") suffer. While Sam had not directed Jenny to do anything that would violate any professional rules or subject her to discipline, Jenny began to have a bad feeling "in her gut" after continuously following Sam's directives.

Sam's directives were aimed at intentionally making Jim's life difficult and to increase the costs and burden on Jim. Sam was angry because Jim took advantage of him in a business dealing and was willing to spare no expense to "teach Jim a lesson." One day, Sam emailed Jenny and directed her to file a motion in the then-pending lawsuit against Jim, and to attach to the motion embarrassing personal documents and private photographs of Jim. These embarrassing materials had little relevance to the lawsuit and if Jenny filed them with the court, they would become public record and would be accessible to anyone. Sam's email provided a detailed plan for incorporating the embarrassing materials as exhibits into an otherwise relevant motion so that the documents and photographs could be filed by Jenny in a way that could be argued as being for a legitimate purpose.

Jenny did not feel good about following Sam's directive and so did not immediately respond to Sam's email. Instead, she brainstormed possible ways to handle the conflict between what her client wanted her to do and what she felt was the right thing to do. After some thought, she decided that the best way to handle the situation was to explain to Sam that the judge would see through the "guise" of legitimacy and recognize that the filing of the embarrassing materials was motivated by spite, and that if the judge suspected Sam of acting out of spite that it would hurt the long-term chances of a successful outcome for his case.

Before relaying this information to the client, Jenny first set up a meeting with her senior partner who agreed and supported her response to Sam. She then responded to Sam's email explaining her position, that her senior partner agreed, and her rationale for not filing the embarrassing materials along with the motion. She offered to set up a meeting to discuss further with Sam if he desired. While Sam expressed disappointment with her decision, he understood and let the matter drop.

In the preceding example, Jenny was able to successfully leverage her experience and specialized knowledge as an attorney and her relationship with her senior partner to develop a strategy to respond to an improper client directive. She was able to recognize that she was not required to follow all client directives, especially as to matters of case strategy, and to explain to the client how what he wanted to do would harm him in the long run. In other words, Jenny was able to leverage the client's own self-interest to get to the outcome she wanted.

Developing Strategies Utilizing GVV Methods in the Legal Industry

There are many values at stake in the legal industry. For an advocate, the values of zealousness, respect, responsibility, integrity, and honesty are regularly at stake. A failure in any of these domains could lead to the undermining of trust in a legal professional or the field of law as an institution for ensuring justice. Developing strategies aimed at ensuring these values are voiced in advocacy contexts involves, among other things, considering the audience, determining the appropriate communication medium or style, gathering information and data to support one's position, charting incremental steps to attaining the goal, and evaluating the risks to decipher ways to limit or negate the fallout.[9] In legal practice, much time is spent gathering the information and data (including facts and law) to support the arguments, but the other aspects of developing a strategy also play an important role in voicing values in advocacy contexts.

Knowing your audience is a key factor in developing a successful strategy for voicing values in advocacy contexts. If the audience is a judge, a prudent advocate will read the judge's prior opinions, talk to others in the legal community about the judge, learn the judge's political affiliations and views, and craft an argument tailored to the presiding judge. In jury contexts, the voir dire selection can provide some information about the contours of the audience, as can continuously reading the jurors' reactions as the trial progresses. When advocating to opposing counsel, one should keep in mind that there are many different types of people in this world, and many different types of attorneys. Knowing each attorney's reputation and history will influence how one deals with that person. Learning about one's audience and tailoring one's voice to that audience is an important factor in implementing one's strategy.

The medium and style of communication should also be considered and evaluated. Whether one or multiple attorneys will appear at a hearing for a motion or for trial, whether information sought by opposing counsel should be sought through letter or a phone call, whether and what exhibits to include and the format of them, and how best to communicate with the stakeholders (email, telephone, etc.) all play a role in deciphering the appropriate strategy for advocacy. The style of communication may also include whether to posit questions, make statements, or utilize some combination approach. Not only the means but also the manner of communication, including the inflection in one's voice, assertiveness, and other qualities also play a role in stylistically advocating for one's client's interests.

Gathering information and data in advocacy contexts can be done in a variety of ways. In litigation contexts, the facts are typically gathered through discovery mechanisms such as interrogatories, requests for documents, requests for admissions, and depositions. Interviews and affidavits are also regularly utilized. The law is gathered through legal research and interpretations. The facts and law are skillfully combined to support an argument. The gathering of information and effectively displaying information are both key facets of implementing a strategy for voicing values in advocacy settings.

Charting incremental steps to attaining one's goal is also an effective component of implementing a strategy. Steps can be utilized to gather information in support of one's claims or defenses. Through deposition, for instance, one may uncover documents which are subsequently requested through document requests. While information may not be readily available, a multipronged strategy may be used to find relevant information. Charting a course and thinking of things as a smaller piece of a whole puzzle may allow one to conceptualize new approaches to case management and oversight. For instance, by thinking ahead, unfavorable evidence uncovered in discovery may be earmarked for a subsequent pretrial motion, such as a motion in limine, that requests the evidence be barred from consideration at trial.

Finally, risk analysis and mitigation can be utilized in every aspect of advocacy from case and client selection through trial and appeal. Analyzing the risks associated with any action taken on behalf of a client and examining potential consequences and reactions by other stakeholders, and anticipating the response or next steps, can mitigate harm to case and client. Some risks that should regularly be prepared for are the risks associated with the busy schedules of judges in contemporary times. Presiding judges are not always educated in the particular area of litigation of each case and do not always have time to read the filings before a hearing. This is largely due to the pressures and busy dockets of judges, and other factors such as the moving of judges across fields and specializations (thereby causing judges to learn new fields). An advocate should prepare for this to occur and be ready to educate a judge in the law and tell the judge about the case, even if papers have already been filed.

While every case is unique, utilizing these factors as part of devising strategies for voicing values in advocacy contexts can help lead to success. All the while, remembering that "it is important to tell a story to ourselves that positions both the failures and the successes as part of a process in building a voice."[10] Even if not successful in the implementation of strategies for voicing values, one can choose to learn from the failures to decipher new ways of doing things when the next opportunity arises. Through the process of self-reflection, one can devise new and better approaches to effectuating the core values of the legal field.

The core values of advocacy, including honesty, integrity, zealousness, respect, and responsibility, can effectively be voiced in adversarial contexts. If one is speaking truth, one must sometimes speak loudly and correct the misrepresentations of others. While a signed affidavit is enough for some attorneys to bring a lawsuit, others engage in more comprehensive due diligence by gathering evidence and facts that support the allegation before bringing a claim. Some who just "cover themselves" by relying solely on the client's affidavit may be more willing to engage questionable cases so long as there are paying clients.

Defining the Core Values of Advocacy

Attorneys who engage in legal practice are constantly faced with opportunities for dishonesty, to engage in bad faith activities, and to violate the core values of advocacy. Attorneys are also faced with opposing counsels who violate the core values of advocacy. Prior to scripting strategies for voicing the core values of advocacy in various contexts, first, an examination of the meaning of each of these values is merited.

Honesty is not an unbridled value, but itself has limits. Honesty entails abiding by certain precepts such as telling the truth, keeping one's promises, and following through on one's agreements. The converse, dishonesty, could involve not abiding by these precepts, however, not all instances of not abiding by these precepts constitutes dishonesty. While generally one should tell the truth, there are instances when not doing so would not be dishonest. In response to the question from a spouse, "do these pants make me look fat?" one should think carefully about the appropriate response and the results that too honest a response may have. Certain act utilitarian views do encourage lying when doing so would promote the greatest good for all involved in a situation. While one should keep one's promises and follow through on one's agreements, sometimes extenuating circumstances may lead one to fail to do so.

In advocacy contexts, honesty entails much of the same as in general societal contexts, but a bit more strategy is involved. There are many ways of looking at the same set of circumstances. Providing an honest analysis of those circumstances and presenting those circumstances to a court sometimes involve using language to tell a story which appears most favorable to one's client by utilizing the most favorable available facts. Surviving motions for summary judgment, for instance, involves disputing material facts which are painted by the opposition in a way that is most favorable to their client. To create a genuine dispute, one must similarly paint the available facts in a way that promotes client interests. One must use one's best judgment to decipher when a client or witness is being honest and create a convincing narrative through storytelling to survive the motion.[11] Consider the following example of the witness affidavit and how honesty may be achieved in practice.

THE WITNESS AFFIDAVIT

Damion, a seasoned litigation attorney, has long recognized that clients and other witnesses will sign affidavits (sometimes called "certifications" or "declarations") that are written by attorneys in his firm without making any revisions or corrections to the affidavits. He has seen other attorneys in his firm use this to their advantage by "inflating" the factual content of affidavits to benefit the cases they are working on. These attorneys insert exaggerations and overstatements into the affidavits that tend to support the claims they are making, and then ask witnesses to review and sign them.

Rarely does a witness revise an affidavit written by one of the firm's attorneys. To the contrary, most of the time each witness signs off on the affidavit, swearing to its truth including the truth of the inflated statements. Often these inflated affidavits are used to support or overcome summary judgment motions, and ultimately contribute to the firm's ability to have cases filed against their clients dismissed or to the settlement of claims.

Damion has repeatedly discussed his observations with other attorneys in his firm and they all agree that it is each witness's responsibility to ensure the accuracy of the facts in the affidavit. The consensus is that the attorneys drafting the affidavits are responsible for framing the facts truthfully, but in the way most beneficial to the client and case and if there are any inaccuracies in that framing, the witness is responsible for bringing them to the firm's attention and correcting them before signing. However, many of the attorneys also felt uneasy about how frequently the witnesses just "rubber stamped" the affidavits.

As a result of the conversations with his colleagues, Damion and the other attorneys in the firm decided to develop a standard form email which is now sent along with every draft affidavit. The email relays to each witness that he or she *not only can but should* correct any misstatements or overstatements in the affidavit, and that it is of the utmost importance that everything in the affidavit is accurate. The email encourages each witness to be honest and to maintain the integrity of the judicial process by carefully reviewing the affidavit and that the witness has an obligation to notify the firm of any errors.

Through conversations with colleagues about an ethical issue, Damion was able to recognize that others in his firm felt similarly uncomfortable about witness affidavits and, consequently, they were able to work together to devise a method to promote honesty in the process while simultaneously ensuring that the facts were framed in a truthful yet beneficial way for their clients. While attorneys have an obligation to draft truthful affidavits, mistakes and misunderstandings are inevitable. The collaborative approach employed by Damion and his colleagues encourages witnesses to take responsibility for what they sign, and for the attorneys to take responsibility for ensuring the accurate factual content of affidavits.

Integrity is a value that is closely related to honesty but involves a moral fortitude that goes beyond the precepts of honesty. Integrity is a way of being that involves living a life in accordance with one's values and principles. Many of the greatest leaders in history are revered for living their lives with integrity. Effective advocacy does involve integrity. However, practical wisdom and prudence are also involved in advocating with integrity. Many a lawyer with integrity has believed the wrong client or made other mistakes in the litigation process that tarnished their reputations. Learning to discern truth is part of the process of becoming an effective advocate. Regardless of mistakes made, one should strive to embrace integrity by living one's moral principles in every aspect of life, advocacy, and legal practice.

Zealousness is perhaps a value best understood within an Aristotelian framework. Aristotle described moral virtues as existing as a mean between two extremes.[12] In each situation, one ought to examine all the circumstances to decipher where on a spectrum virtuous activity lies. On either end of the spectrum are extremes which are sometimes referred to as "vices," and in the middle is the virtuous activity. By engaging in virtuous activity repeatedly, Aristotle says, it eventually becomes a part of one's character and becomes easier to recognize in each situation.[13] Zealous representation similarly lies as a mean between the extremes of overzealousness and overly passive representation. Zealously representing a client involves finding the appropriate balance between these two extremes in any given situation, and, through practice, proper zealousness is attained in advocacy. It involves reading a situation to determine when to speak up and when to stay quiet, when to assert one's position and when to listen, and when to push harder and when to let go.

Respect involves providing due regard to other people's views, feelings, opinion, and perspectives because they are human beings, giving due regard to traditions of the legal system and procedures of courts, and giving due regard to cultural and professional traditions. One may not agree with a judge's decision, with opposing counsel's position, or with other viewpoints, but one should show respect to their views. Demeaning and derogatory remarks are disrespectful. Respecting others entails a degree of empathy, understanding, and conceptualizing walking in the shoes of another. Defense attorneys are hired to defend their clients. Plaintiff's attorneys are hired to assert the rights of their clients. Judges must balance these competing interests in as equitable a manner as possible, given the law and facts of a case. Respect for the legal system involves not bringing frivolous lawsuits and engaging in due diligence in representation. However, as the following scenario illustrates, such decisions are often complicated by the realities of a particular situation.

THE POTENTIALLY PROBLEMATIC CLIENT

Melinda was a senior associate in a busy law firm who was approached by a potential new client, Jessica, regarding a matter of unsettled law. In her jurisdiction, there were conflicting lower court decisions about how the statute at issue in Jessica's case should be interpreted. Melinda was at first excited about the prospect of bringing Jessica's lawsuit. The potential for testing the appellate court on this issue of unsettled law and the media coverage that would follow on this important issue was enticing to Melinda whose first thought was that "this could be the case that gets me promoted to partner."

Melinda conducted extensive research and learned that most of the lower courts tended to interpret the statute in the way needed for Jessica to win her case. She also learned that one of the lower court judges who wrote the leading opinion on this same interpretation was recently appointed to the appellate court that would ultimately hear and decide Jessica's case. Melinda felt great about the potential for success, and had Jessica execute an attorney retention agreement and pay a retainer fee.

A few days after Jessica signed the retainer agreement and paid the fee, one of Melinda's colleagues emailed Melinda several online articles from a local media source about the client, Jessica. According to these articles, Jessica was a "serial plaintiff" who repeatedly represented herself in frivolous lawsuits against various defendants. One article quoted a court's opinion dismissing a case filed by Jessica which said that Jessica had filed the case "with the intention of harassing the defendant." Another article accused Jessica of "committing fraud on the court" against the very same defendant that Melinda's firm was hired to sue.

Melinda felt uneasy after reading these articles and began pondering what she should do. Adding complexity to the situation, the statute of limitations for filing the claim on behalf of Jessica was going to expire in less than a month. Melinda feared that if she withdrew after being retained, and before filing the lawsuit, that she and her firm would face a malpractice claim from Jessica.

Melinda decided to bring the issue to the attention of the firm's senior partners. In collaboration, they decided to hold an immediate meeting with the firm's senior partners, Melinda, and Jessica. In this meeting, Melinda discussed the news articles with Jessica and how her history of fraud, harassment, and serial lawsuits was unknown to the firm at the time of signing the retainer. They explained that considering Jessica's history (and particularly her history with this defendant), that they believed her case would not be successful, and so they would be withdrawing from her representation. The attorneys prepared a carefully crafted release agreement which in bold letters informed Jessica of the statute of limitations on her claims and requested that Jessica sign the release. Unfortunately, Jessica refused to sign the release, and stormed out of the office in a fit of rage.

When the release approach did not work, Melinda and the firm's partners adjusted to Jessica's response. They then crafted a carefully worded letter explaining the circumstance of their withdrawal from representation. In that letter, they documented Jessica's history of fraud, history with this defendant, the unsettled law, her refusal to sign the release, and that she had been repeatedly informed of the statute of limitations on her claims. They returned her full retainer payment and advised her to immediately retain another firm for a second opinion.

While time was lost on Jessica's case and there continued to be a risk of a frivolous malpractice claim against Melinda's firm, the attorneys in the firm documented everything to protect the firm's interest in face of a potentially problematic client and adjusted their approach to protect the firm while respecting the integrity of the judicial process.

Being an advocate is itself a great responsibility. Another person's rights, which may include life, liberty, property, or other rights, are at grave risk. The advocate carries the responsibility of protecting these rights in face of an adversary intent on taking them away. This responsibility involves ensuring diligence in representation and doing the best one can under the circumstances of each case. It involves complying with the rules of court, meeting deadlines, communicating effectively with others, and meeting client needs. One should also take responsibility for one's actions and mistakes.

The preceding definitions of the core values of advocacy are merely starting points for explaining what these values mean in advocacy contexts, and the application of these values will vary based on each situation. Like the Aristotelian mean, one must find the appropriate balance within and among these values in each situation.

Pre-scripting Strategies for Voicing the Core Values of Advocacy

Advocacy is conducted in an adversarial environment wherein viewpoints, motives, and incentives are in conflict. For some, there is a significant temptation to hide information that harms one's case. For some, there is a temptation to lie in court regarding issues that cannot be proven or disproven. For some, there is a temptation to utilize the judicial system for revenge or out of spite. Engaging in any of these actions undermines justice and violates the core values of advocacy. The most difficult situations arise when the opposition engages in these types of deceitful behaviors. The following paragraphs prescript techniques for voicing values when the opposition engages in such actions.

Adversaries that fail to disclose harmful information often do so either with the intent to never disclose it or, sometimes, with the intent to disclose the information at a strategic point in time, after extensive and expensive motions practice. The latter route involves the ongoing song and dance of deficiency letters, motions to compel, and court orders. Some attorneys wait until the opposition has expended considerable resources trying to get the information from the other side before finally disclosing it at a time when the risk of sanctions remains minimal. In most courts the awarding of attorney's fees for a motion to compel is discretionary, and, in practice, are not always awarded. This "song and dance" produces billable hours for all involved attorneys, and clients suffer the increased bill because of it.

This common practice or "song and dance," if you will, regularly occurs in litigation contexts, and is generally accepted by attorneys as a matter of course. The reality is that this common practice negatively impacts the clients, while benefiting attorneys. Trying to voice values may prove troublesome in face of the profit motive and self-interest of attorneys in need of satisfying billable hour quotas. Yet, because of the powerful incentives cutting against integrity in this instance, it is ever so much more important to prescript exercises to evaluate how to change this practice.

Imagine a single mother fighting her way through a divorce from the breadwinner husband who is engaging in vexatious litigation and withholding financial information. The single mother is struggling to make ends meet, living with her parents, and fighting a battle against the more powerful moneyed party with the stress from the divorce magnified by the financial strain caused by her husband's attorney's tactics. This mother is suffering tremendously already, and this strain is increased when her husband's attorney refuses to produce financial documents that are required to be produced, thereby increasing the costs associated with the divorce and the strain on her.

As in the preceding example, the more moneyed party often intends to cause strife for the weaker party with the intention of breaking the party down and causing her to give up the fight. It would be a fruitless exercise for even the most skilled advocate to attempt to voice values to opposing counsel who is engaging in these tactics. Trying to overcome these inequities by pleading to opposing counsel would only reveal the type of weakness the opposition is trying to take advantage of and perhaps even create a sick joy for the moneyed party set on revenge. The inequity of this situation is best mitigated through judicial intervention. A learned judge has observed such tactics and an effective advocate, exercising appropriate zeal, can reveal these inequities and seek relief from a judge. Consider the following example of Amber and how she overcame inequities in the discovery process.

THE OPPOSING COUNSEL WHO DOES NOT PRODUCE

Amber was an associate attorney who was assigned to work on discovery issues in one of the firm's cases. Opposing counsel in this matter, Ross, was a very experienced litigator who worked for a very politically connected law firm with personal and professional ties to many of the judges in the county. Ross's law firm was one of the oldest and most respected in the region, and Ross was known for being "untouchable," and for taking a lot of liberty in his cases knowing that due to his and his firm's political connections, he would not likely face sanctions by the judges that his firm helped put on the bench. His firm was often hired to represent regional governments, local politicians, and upper-level governmental employees.

Amber reviewed all the discovery requests her firm sent Ross's firm in this case, and reviewed Ross's responses to them which included boilerplate objections to every single discovery request, and a refusal to produce the information and documents requested. Amber's firm already sent multiple deficiency letters to Ross, and he still did not respond. The firm also filed a motion to compel the discovery requests, to which Ross did not respond, and the motion to compel was granted without opposition. Amber was baffled. Having recently graduated law school, she never imagined she'd see anything like this. She was taught in law school that lawyers were required to follow the rules of court and court orders. Ross had completely ignored the rules of court and the court order compelling him to provide the discovery responses, and she didn't know what else she could do.

Thousands of dollars had already been billed to her firm's client for the letters and motion relating to recovering these discovery responses which should have been provided many months ago. She attempted to call Ross several times, but he repeatedly refused to take and return her calls. Amber recognized that the judge would need to intervene, so began crafting a motion for sanctions against Ross. She was nervous because of Ross's reputation as "untouchable" and his political ties to the court. She felt powerless and fearful but mustered the courage to fight for her client. She spent many hours preparing a detailed motion, which, as an associate of the firm, was required to bill to her client. The preparation of her motion cost her client thousands more dollars. She then filed the motion for sanctions, and less than a week before oral argument for the motion was scheduled, Ross finally produced the discovery items he was previously ordered to produce.

When oral argument came, Ross told the judge that everything had already been produced, and Amber's requests for sanctions and to recover the thousands of dollars spent by her client trying to recover these discovery responses were denied by the judge. Although Amber lost the motion for sanctions, she was nonetheless able to recover the evidence that her firm needed to prepare the case toward trial.

While each situation is unique, and often may be addressed through strategy and skillful intervention by the advocate, correcting this continuing problem may require a rethinking of the institutionalized discovery process. The process by which advocates conduct discovery is so engrained in the American common law system that it is often accepted as a "matter of fact" by attorneys engaged in the process. The key to equalizing the inequities apparent in the above scenario requires reform of the court rules governing discovery and motions to compel. The rules, as they are written, are too often leveraged to provide parties and representing counsel many opportunities to skirt the intent of the rules for their own benefit.[14] The process of institutional change begins with rethinking the rules by which discovery are conducted and devising ways by which these inequities can be reduced in practice. Until such institutional level changes are made, counsel must continue to devise unique strategies for voicing values when inequities present themselves during a case.

While some deficiencies with the system may be addressed at an institutional level, one cannot control the individualized circumstances of parties or witnesses engaging in deception. Addressing deceit in litigation contexts requires an advocate to collect evidence that undermines the credibility of the deceiver. This could be through certifications or affidavits of others who contradict what the deceiver says, credible evidence that calls into question the words of the deceiver, or some combination of the preceding. The way the advocate presents this evidence, whether through impeachment or on the papers will vary circumstantially, but what an effective advocate must do is present the truth to the court so that justice does prevail.

There are so many dishonest people in the world today with varying motivations for deceiving others. Sometimes these dishonest people collude together to script their stories into a seemingly coherent narrative of facts. When multiple people are involved in illegal acts, they often create jointly fabricated narratives to protect themselves from civil liability or criminal culpability. Such collusion is inherently difficult to overcome. In more extreme cases, the deceivers begin to believe their own fabrications, and live in a world of illusion. Yet, if one person comes forward and speaks the truth the illusion begins to unravel at least for those who did not drink the metaphorical Kool-Aid. Oh yeah … it's a challenge for an advocate to pierce through collusion to present the truth, but it can be done.

THE DECEITFUL OPPOSING PARTY

Jaemin is a plaintiff's attorney who specializes in civil rights and employment litigation. He is well known and respected as one of the best in his field in the region and state. He owns his own boutique practice and employs several associates and other staff. Given particularly the sensitive nature of many of the lawsuits he has filed, which often involve issues of racism and bigotry, he has observed that defendants regularly deny all allegations made against them. The denials typically begin with the Answer to the Complaint. In the Answer, the defendants deny all but the most insignificant allegations of the Complaint. As the case progresses, Jaemin has observed that defendants tend to deny everything which cannot unequivocally be proven by the available evidence.

As the plaintiff's attorney, Jaemin has the burden of proving the elements of his claims, and the tendency of defendants to deny everything makes this burden difficult. As a result, in his practice area, Jaemin collects and utilizes circumstantial evidence to prove the civil rights violations at issue. Such evidence often includes contradicting reasons for actions or shifting rationales, inappropriate remarks or statements, mistreatment of others who are similarly situated, violations of internal policies, statistical evidence, and/or a showing of insufficient or missing documentation. Once Jaemin has the circumstantial evidence in hand, he will often seek to attain direct evidence of a violation through questioning witnesses in depositions about the circumstantial evidence until an admission is made. In other instances, Jaemin collects enough circumstantial evidence to show the denials are untrue even in the absence of direct evidence. In face of deceit, Jaemin collects circumstantial evidence which he, in turn, utilizes to reveal that the denials made by defendants are untrue.

As the previous example reveals, in some cases the truth can be uncovered through skillful and strategic lawyering. In face of a culpable party that denies any wrongdoing, gathering and using circumstantial evidence is one strategy for overcoming deceit by the other party.

The problem of deceit is closely tied to the problem of frivolous or spitefully filed claims. While there are prohibitions on attorneys filing frivolous claims, and many states have laws prohibiting litigants from filing frivolous claims, once a frivolous complaint has been filed, it creates stress, unnecessary costs, and a protracted court process.[15] Unfortunately, there is no easy way to decipher between good and bad faith in litigation, and some cases that never should have been filed in the first place will proceed on the merits. Deceitful attorneys learn ways to manipulate the circumstances to attain their goals, even if lacking a legitimate basis in law and fact. They know what to tell their clients to say, and vexatious clients are not fearful to sign on to get their revenge or potential gain from a lawsuit. The sad reality is that if there is the potential to gain and little to lose, then some will opt to file a lawsuit. "Sure, I'll take your money," a deceitful lawyer may think and then take a case from a paying client that causes insufferable harm to others.

Advocates have a responsibility to ensure that their clients are protected from frivolous claims. Court rules provide some deterrence to such claims, but the procedure by which one goes about recovering for a frivolous action is itself a lengthy and arduous process. Victims of vexatious litigation should not have to go through so much turmoil to have their rights vindicated, but a better option is not easily apparent. While it is easy to say that frivolous actions should not be brought, they are sometimes brought because of client deceit, attorney manipulation, or a combination of the two. There are economic consequences to these claims, as well as psychological pain and opportunities lost because of the time spent defending a baseless action.

Advocates have a responsibility not only to protect their clients from frivolous claims, but also to avoid filing frivolous claims in the first place. While it is easy to rationalize bringing claims by a paying client, thinking along the lines of "if I don't do it someone else will," some attorneys bring these claims that cause reputational damage to the filing attorney and harm to others. As John Stuart Mill put forth, we are free to act as we desire but can be legitimately prohibited from acting when doing so harms others.[16] There are limits indeed to what can be done in litigation contexts, and advocates should respect those limits regardless of the potential for momentary economic gain.

A FAILED ATTEMPT AT TURNING DOWN A CLIENT

Bud was a new associate attorney who struggled to find a job and finally landed his first position in a law firm. The firm's owner, Chase, was not well-reputed in the legal community, but Bud needed income and experience so felt he had to take this opportunity to gain experience with the hope of eventually finding employment at a better firm.

A few weeks into his new position, Chase asked Bud to join him in a meeting with a potential new client, who was a very wealthy businessman and was seeking a law firm to represent him in a lawsuit against his former business partner. During the meeting, the potential client explained his case to Chase and Bud, and Chase quoted the potential client the firm's hourly fees and retainer requirements. Chase also explained that there were no guarantees of a successful outcome.

After the meeting, Chase and Bud talked and Chase asked Bud what he thought about the case. Bud explained that he thought the case was very weak and it was not in the potential client's best interest to bring the lawsuit and that he thought it would be a waste of the client's money. Bud also explained that he did not think the potential client came across as credible or trustworthy. Chase agreed with Bud's assessment.

A few days later, Chase emailed Bud, and told him that the potential client had retained the firm, and that Bud was assigned to represent the client in his case and to prepare a Complaint against the client's former business partner. Bud was surprised to receive this email because he thought Chase had agreed that the case was not a strong one, and that the firm shouldn't take it. Bud then walked over to Chase's office to discuss.

Chase explained to Bud that the client is wealthy and paid a high retainer amount and agreed to a high hourly fee. The client also executed the firm's standard retainer agreement which disclaims any guarantees or promises of a successful outcome. Chase told Bud to get started on drafting the client's Complaint and to "take your time on it," implying that Bud should spend a lot of time billing hours on this client's Complaint.

Bud did not feel good about this situation but felt as though Chase had made his decision, and there was nothing else he could say that would change Chase's mind. Bud did not want to lose his first legal job, possibly ruining his future career, and so prepared the Complaint. However, he spent only the amount of time needed to prepare the Complaint and did not spend any unnecessary time on it.

In the meantime, Bud began looking for another job because he realized that he would not be able to continue to live by his values while working for Chase. Although Bud was not able to effectuate change through his attempts to voice values, Chase recognized a bad situation and that the culture of the firm did not match with his own values. He therefore made the choice to adhere to his values as best he could while working for Chase and to seek alternative employment.

In the preceding examples, integrity and honesty are identified as the starting point for effectively undermining harmful discovery practices, as the cornerstone to overcoming deceit in legal contexts, and as the basis for not filing frivolous claims. The lawyer's responsibility to protect her client and others from frivolous claims is explored. It is asserted that there is a need to respect the integrity of the court rules and practices by not leveraging rules in ways inimical to justice. The appropriate balance of zealousness flows through all these examples. The zealous advocate must discover and implement the appropriate strategy for change and voicing values in adversarial contexts. By abiding by the core values of advocacy and reconciling client needs with the values of the advocate and other stakeholders, a lawyer can devise strategies to effectively voice values in adversarial contexts or, when initial attempts at effectuating values fail, to develop alternative solutions that meet the needs of the situation.

Adhering to the core values of advocacy will contribute to building trust with constituents of the legal field. The next chapter, Chapter 5, explores additional techniques that attorneys can employ to build trust with clients and other stakeholders.

Notes

1 See generally Mary C. Gentile, *Giving Voice to Values: How to Speak Your Mind When You Know What's Right* (2010).

2 Joseph D. Jamail, Advocacy and Lawyers and their Role, 47 *Baylor L. Rev.* 1159 (1995).

3 Lee E. Teitelbaum, The Advocate's Role in the Legal System, 6 *N.M. L. Rev.* 1, 16 (1976).

4 Mary C. Gentile, *Giving Voice to Values: How to Speak Your Mind When You Know What's Right*, 194 (2010).

5 Carolyn Plump, *Giving Voice to Values in the Legal Profession: Effective Advocacy with Integrity* (2018).

6 *Id.* at 15.

7 Robert Feldman, *Professionalism and Values in Law Practice*, viii (2020).

8 This is the first of many illustrative scenarios in this book. Most of the illustrative scenarios are composites that are pulled from the author's years of legal practice experience, and others are fictional examples. The author made every effort to maintain anonymity in all illustrative scenarios

by changing names, places, details, and facts to such a considerable
degree that there should not be any resemblance to actual persons or
events. The illustrations are intended to reveal how the *Giving Voice to
Values* strategies and theory discussed in this book may be implemented.
Each situation is unique, and the context of the situation, values, local
professional rules, laws, and other environment factors should be
considered before implementing any strategy.

9   Carolyn Plump, *Giving Voice to Values in the Legal Profession: Effective
Advocacy with Integrity*, 18–19 (2018).

10   Mary C. Gentile, *Giving Voice to Values: How to Speak Your Mind When You
Know What's Right*, 168 (2010).

11   ABA Model Rule 3.3 provides that "(a) A lawyer shall not knowingly: (1)
make a false statement of fact or law to a tribunal or fail to correct a
false statement of material fact or law previously made to the tribunal
by the lawyer..." See Model Rule 3.3, American Bar Association, https://
www.americanbar.org/groups/professional_responsibility/publications/
model_rules_of_professional_conduct/rule_3_3_candor_toward_
the_tribunal/

12   Aristotle, *The Nicomachean Ethics*, 39 (trans. David Ross, 1998).

13   Aristotle, *The Nicomachean Ethics*, 28–39 (trans. David Ross, 1998).

14   See, e.g., F.R.C.P. 37.

15   See, e.g., F.R.C.P. 11, N.J. Ct. R. 1:4–8, & N.J.S.A. 2A:15–59.1.

16   John Stuart Mill, *On Liberty*, 68 (Penguin ed., 1974) (1859).

5

BUILDING TRUST IN ATTORNEY RELATIONSHIPS

Embracing the core values of advocacy is part of the process of building trust in the attorney-client relationship, but it is only a portion of what is required to successfully build trust with one's clients. The societal perception that lawyers are not trustworthy can be overcome with cognizance and continuous effort to build trust with one's clients. Building trust with clients allows clients to feel more comfortable confiding in their attorneys, thereby allowing attorneys to gather all the information they need to effectively litigate client matters. Trust has other instrumental benefits including creating a client base that is more likely to provide referrals to the trusted attorney. Yet trust reaches beyond the attorney-client relationship to relationships with all stakeholders including the general public.

Overview of Trust

The concept of trust has been examined by the layperson and philosopher alike. Many people examine trust in terms of relationships, and

DOI: 10.4324/9780429507847-8

quite frequently in terms of personal relationships. Trusting one's significant other or friends on some levels does not mean there is trust on all levels. One may trust another to show up on time, to be honest, or to maintain secrets but not to babysit one's children or to pay back borrowed money. Trust is something that can be given, earned, lost, or regained. There can be no love without trust, but not all trust involves love. Trust involves interpersonal relationships and various people are inclined to trust or distrust others. Few trust strangers, some are more likely to trust others who are met through those already trusted, and some tend to distrust.

Lawyers tend to be distrusted. Earning the trust of client, court, and others in the legal community takes time, effort, and the establishment of a reputation for being trustworthy. Like the graduating college student beginning life indebted with student loans, lawyers begin the quest for establishing a positive reputation "in the red," so to speak, because of societal perceptions that lawyers cannot be trusted. To go from "the red" to "the black" and turn from a perceived untrustworthy lawyer to a lawyer who is perceived as trustworthy takes time. One story describes "Black Friday" as the day that companies finally go from the red to the black, that is, begin making a profit for the year.[1] It takes the majority of the year to turn that profit and similarly it could take the majority of one's career to be perceived as trustworthy. Black Friday comes the day after Thanksgiving, which is celebrated in the United States on the fourth Thursday of November, or after most of the year is concluded. While one would hope that it does not take most of a lifetime to establish oneself as a trustworthy lawyer, it is not something which is immediately or even easily accomplished.

Business ethicist, Tim Fort, developed a tripartite vision of how businesses can build trust through establishing "a set of behaviors, attitudes, and sentiments" which tend to ensure legitimacy and sustainability in business contexts.[2] His model involves promoting three types of trust within an organization: Hard Trust, Real Trust, and Good Trust. This chapter examines these three types of trust and how they can be adapted to the unique features of the adversarial context of legal practice. Fort's tripartite vision of trust can guide legal practitioners to build trust not only with clients but also with court, opposing counsel, and all stakeholders of the profession.

Hard Trust

Hard trust involves compliance with laws and other mandatory rules, such as the Rules of Professional Conduct. It is the kind of trust that lawyers most frequently embark to earn, and failures in this dimension can lead to catastrophe. In the legal field, much of engendering hard trust involves compliance with laws and the Rules of Professional Conduct within the relevant jurisdiction. Although there are variations among states, the ABA Model Rules of Professional Conduct are adopted by most states in one form or another and lay out the baseline compliance requirements for attorneys. Included among these rules are obligations of competence, diligence, communication, maintaining a reasonable fee, confidentiality, avoiding conflicts of interest, safekeeping of property, candor, fairness, impartiality, truthfulness, and respect for rights of others.[3]

The Rules of Professional Conduct function to ensure public confidence in the legal field, by providing baseline obligations that attorneys cannot deviate from. The rules further curb the accumulation of power that could otherwise come with a law license by placing boundaries on permissible action. The purpose of many laws and professional rules is to prevent abuses of the powerful at the expense of more vulnerable populations. Model Rules 1.1, 1.3, 1.5, and 1.6 all are intended to protect the public from attorney abuses.

Model Rule 1.1 requires a lawyer to be competent when representing clients. This requires "the legal knowledge, skill, thoroughness and preparation reasonably necessary for the representation."[4] This rule similarly provides a baseline protection for clients from lawyers who lack expertise in the area of law they are hired to work in. However, the comments to the rule allow lawyers to accept representation when competence may be achieved by adequate preparation or by associating with lawyers in the field with the established competence.[5] This rule provides guidance to lawyers who seek to expand their practice areas or to otherwise engage in cases they may not otherwise usually take. The guidance is aimed at protecting the general public from incompetent representation.

Model Rule 1.3 requires a lawyer to act with reasonable diligence and promptness when representing clients.[6] However, the "lawyer's duty to act with reasonable diligence does not require the use of offensive tactics or preclude the treating of all persons involved in the legal process with courtesy and respect."[7] This qualification makes clear that there are limits to the scope of diligent representation and those limits include engaging in offensive and disrespectful behavior – something which many lawyers should take note of – a qualification which protects both the general public and others engaged in legal practice.

Model Rule 1.5 prohibits attorneys from charging unreasonable fees.[8] Rule 1.5 protects the vulnerable general population from being charged unreasonable amounts by the elite that possess legal licenses and represent others. Without this protection for the general public, the already significant fees for legal representation would likely be higher. Those who really need legal services would either face an inability to attain them or the metaphorical "poor house" when seeking to vindicate their rights.

Model Rule 1.6 ensures that client information is kept confidential unless the client gives informed consent or disclosure is otherwise authorized by the rule.[9] Rule 1.6 protects the general population from the exposure of their personal information which is entrusted with counsel. However, confidentiality also has limits including when the client is utilizing the lawyer's services to assist with committing a crime or fraud.[10] In such instances, a lawyer is permitted to disclose information as reasonably necessary to prevent the crime or fraud. This carve-out to the general requirement of maintaining confidential information is similarly intended to protect the general public from misuses of the attorney-client relationship to perpetrate illegal activities.

The Rules of Professional Conduct are mandatory for attorneys. Violating the rules can lead to sanctions, which reduces trust in the sanctioned attorney. To build hard trust, an attorney should comply with laws, regulations, and other rules including the Rules of Professional Conduct. The following examples reveal the consequences that may arise when attorneys violate the Rules of Professional Conduct.

The story of Stan represents the extreme case of an attorney who was engaged in many violations of the professional rules. His advantage-seeking and dishonesty were apparent from early in the relationship, but the newly minted attorneys, including John, who worked for him felt powerless to rectify the wrongs. There was little they could do but leave the firm and take a monetary loss. Had John not left the firm when he did, he too may have been investigated for violations of the professional rules and potentially sanctioned or even disbarred. The next story, of Barry, represents an area involving more shades of gray.

THE NEWLY MINTED ATTORNEY: PART I

As a lawyer who graduated during the great recession, John entered the legal market at a time of great uncertainty. There was upheaval in the legal industry, and jobs were scarce. There were few opportunities for newly minted attorneys with little practical experience. As student loans came due and mortgage payments and other bills continued, John had little choice but to take a position in a start-up law firm on a percentage-of-fee basis. John had no set salary, no benefits, and the owner of this start-up had little, if any, experience in general practice. This lawyer, Stan, hired a cadre of young attorneys on similar percentage-bases, and put them to work earning only a percentage of what the client paid, with extreme uncertainty about income and prospects of this firm.

As the weeks turned into months, Stan began to express that he was having financial problems and said he would need to defer part of John's payment until later in the month. This deferral of payment continued until thousands upon thousands of dollars were owed, and John was continuously working without receiving his fully agreed upon share of payments. When John asked to be paid in full, Stan became aggressive which led to a severing of the relationship.

Before this time, however, John observed that Stan would regularly misrepresent things, he even asked John to lie for him, and he would give instructions to the attorneys working for him that were contrary to the procedures of the courts. When John left the firm, he was owed thousands upon thousands of dollars, a portion of which he did eventually receive, but was left with a foul taste in his mouth for legal practice. If this is the practice of law, John realized that he was in the wrong profession. This experience impacted John for many years that followed.

Years later, after John was stable in his career, he discovered that Stan had been disbarred from the practice of law. The Supreme Court of the state affirmed his disbarment for over forty (40) violations of the Rules of Professional Conduct. When John learned of this, he began to reflect on the choices he made and his short stint working for Stan. While John regretted the experience, it was validating to know that someone who had taken advantage of him and others during a time of extreme vulnerability, was, in turn, prohibited from continuing to work in the legal field. The failure to comply with the professional rules led to the demise of Stan's practice, his income, and his reputation as a lawyer in the community.

THE NEWLY MINTED ATTORNEY: PART 2

Sometime after working with Stan, John began working with another law firm which maintained a business-like firm culture and a focus on the firm as a profit-center. This firm was more integrated in the community and offered a better and more consistent income. The owner, Barry, established himself within the local bar associations, politically, and in the right circles. Barry really had a way about him, was a talented rainmaker, and had the voice of a salesman.

At first, Barry was incredibly generous, supportive, and kind. John began as one of his first associates and felt as though he was being taken under his wing. John recalls thinking how fortunate he was to be working in a better environment and with better people. John's income increased, and he became better known in the local legal community. As time went on and Barry's practice grew, he hired other associates, and in his quest for power, prestige, and money, began to lose sight of those who cared the most about him and the firm.

Barry took a compliance approach to ethics, and generally met the baseline requirements of abiding by the professional rules. However, as the pressure increased, his kindness diminished and, he became spitefully cruel at times, threatening, and vengeful. While Barry managed to maintain his practice for many years, and was involved in some disputes with clients, his general baseline of compliance and political connections largely insulated him from losing his license. There were some red flags when working with Barry including his suggesting that John bill clients two hours for every one hour he worked (which John did not do) and his paying his employee, John, a large sum with a check, without withholding taxes (John paid taxes on it). Yet, the firm was integrated in the community and appeared to be gaining traction for success.

However, as Barry's attitude changed, he lost the trust and respect of many who worked with him, the clients who hired him, and many within the community he aimed to serve. Several years after John left the firm, Barry's seemingly minor indiscretions rose to more major problems, and allegations were made against him. Barry was thereafter suspended on an interim basis from the practice of law for, among other reasons, because he appeared to pose a substantial threat of serious harm to the public.

What these two examples display (aside from poor choices in employers) is that hard trust is easily lost when professional rules are violated. Stan's and Barry's names are forever sullied and in this age of the internet, an online search would reveal the disciplinary sanctions. The sanctions will forever impact their ability to build trust with clients and other stakeholders. These examples reveal that violations of professional rules often overlap with violations of societal norms or moral principles.

Real Trust

Real Trust, as explained by Tim Fort, represents the many dimensions of ethical theory and practice including what are commonly referred to as "descriptive ethics" and "normative ethics." Descriptive ethics is said to be about what people in a situation, firm, business, or industry are doing in terms of ethics (the "is"). That is, the ethical practices and approaches that firms are implementing at a given point in time. What firms are doing changes over time, and so while descriptive ethics can be informative and influential, it does not provide adequate guidance to those in the field. The descriptive dimension, however, is helpful to understanding trends, identifying correlations, and for deciphering commonalities among various constituencies. It provides a limited picture of what may be deemed acceptable practices in a situation, firm, business, or industry.

Normative ethics is said to be more about what people in a situation, firm, business, or industry should be doing in terms of ethics (the "ought"). Simply because a percentage or even most firms are, in fact, handling ethical issues in a certain way does not mean that firms should be acting that way. The normative dimension goes beyond descriptive studies of what is happening on the ground at a given time and provides methods for deciphering right from wrong. Normative ethics provides methodologies for making decisions when the laws and rules may technically allow or at least not prohibit behaviors.

Normative ethics includes consideration of, among other principles and concepts, those of justice, rights, duty, utilitarianism, and virtue. While each of these approaches to ethics are traditionally construed to be mutually exclusive of the other, and some may even abuse these theories in post hoc attempts to justify behavior, all approaches, like all religions, contain elements of wisdom. Whether one adheres to the Quran, the Bible, the

Upanishads, or some other religious canon for moral guidance, one can still appreciate that each book contains elements of wisdom in its doctrine. There is overlap in many of the lessons and principles in each of these books and regardless of the zealots pursuing Crusades some principles like the golden rule ("do unto others") span the spectrum of great religions. Each normative theory standing alone paints an incomplete picture of morality.

When trying to build real trust with stakeholders, lawyers should examine all recognizable principles and concepts of normative ethics. Philosophers quibble over whether the consequences of an act or the intentions of the person performing the act make it moral. Such debates embrace an underlying false dichotomy rooted in centuries of Western philosophical analysis. The morality of an action cannot be separated from its intent or the consequences. To this point, it is imperative that lawyers consider both intentions and consequences when attempting to build real trust with stakeholders. In other words, lawyers should examine their motivations for acting as well as the possible consequences that their actions may have on others.

The desire to make money is a common motivation in the legal industry. In many business and economic contexts, the desire to make money is commonly referred to as the "profit motive," and is closely related to conceptions of self-interest.[11] Most recognize that one cannot blindly seek profits without considering how self-interested profit seeking may affect others. There are some instances in legal practice that a lawyer's profit seeking can harm the client. Such instances are often reflected in attorneys not taking the most efficient route to resolve a case, and thereby increasing billable hours. On the other hand, there are instances when a lawyer's profit seeking can help a client. For instance, when there is a contingency fee arrangement and the lawyer is incentivized to recover the largest amount possible for the client so the lawyer can also attain a larger sum on a percentage of recovery basis. In any pursuit of profit, there are inherent ethical, legal, and societal rules that must be adhered to.

Consequentialism involves examining the impact of one's actions on others when evaluating whether one is doing the right thing. Utilitarianism is a type of consequentialism which involves examining the potential consequences on all stakeholders to decipher a course of action or rule that promotes the greatest good for all involved. Many statutes are based on legislative determinations that the greater good of society will be attained by the promulgation of such laws, thereby grounding laws in utilitarian-like justifications. However, in the adversarial context of the practice of law, attempting to base decisions on the greatest good for all involved, including the adversary, is not a feasible method for deciphering the appropriate action. Nevertheless, considering the consequences of one's actions on all stakeholders can be informative as part of a larger process of moral evaluation, which also involves recognizing basic fairness and respect-based obligations even to adversaries. Consider the following example of building trust through examining consequences.

CROWDED OFFICE SPACE

Mia was an experienced legal assistant who worked in a cubicle in a law office. Seven other legal assistants and paralegals shared a large room with Mia for eight to ten hours a day. Each person had a cubicle with four cubicles on one side of the large room and four on the other. Immediately behind Mia was Daphne, who was a very senior paralegal who had been with the firm for over a decade. Mia and Daphne were close friends and regularly chit-chatted throughout the day, talked over their shared cubicle wall, laughed loudly, and disrupted the work of the other six people in the room.

Although Mia and Daphne talked and laughed, they both completed their work in a professional and timely manner. They spent a lot of time in the office and tried to make it a joyful place while simultaneously completing quality work in an efficient way. Although their work was good, some of the others in the room complained to the managing attorney, Mark, about the noise and disruption coming from Daphne and Mia. Others in the room joined in their fun, and talked and laughed with them, but didn't produce as high quality of work and sometimes missed important deadlines.

Mark wants to create a work environment that was joyful and pleasant for everyone. He realized that his staff spends a lot of time in the office, so wanted it to be a good working environment. However, he recognized that the consequences of Mia and Daphne's behavior were detrimental to the other six people who were annoyed or distracted by them, and he needed his team to function efficiently.

Mark ultimately discussed the matter with Mia and Daphne, and how he wanted them to be able to enjoy their work, and appreciated their high quality of work, but didn't want others in the firm to get distracted. Mark gave them the choice of either remaining in their current space and staying quiet or moving their cubicles to a smaller vacant room in the office, which was out of earshot of everyone else. He left it up to Mia and Daphne to make this choice, and they opted to move. After they moved, their work continued to be of high quality and the efficiency of the six who remained in the large room increased. Mark was able to build trust with his employees by recognizing the consequences of his staff's behavior and using choice as a mechanism for change.

Deontology is not as concerned with the consequences of an act, but rather with a person's motivations for acting. In the previous example, Mark focused primarily on the consequences of inaction including the inefficiencies that were arising in the workplace by his employees' behaviors. However, Mark also perceived that he had a duty to promote a joyful workplace for his employees. Deontologists prescribe that moral duty should be the basis for determining right from wrong. Humans are inherently capable of reasoning and can use reason to decipher moral duties under a set of circumstances. One's intention in acting is appropriate when one acts in accordance with moral duties, or, in other words, in accordance with what one is morally obligated to do. The exact contours and scope of duties are debatable, but at least some duties have correlative rights. Life, liberty, property, and the pursuit of happiness are well-established rights within the U.S. system and interfering with those rights often constitutes a violation of moral duty. For instance, when one has a right to life, others have the duty not to interfere with that right to life. When one has a right to basic health, then others have the duty not to interfere with that right. While legal and moral rights often overlap, they are distinct and lawyers striving to build real trust should look beyond the law to ensure that they violate no moral rights, including the inherent right of human dignity. Consider how Maria acted out of duty in the following scenario.

THE GOOD-HEARTED ATTORNEY

Maria was an attorney and an advocate for the equal rights of women. She was known for successfully representing women in business and employment in very high-profile cases which garnered extensive media coverage. Most of her clients in recent times were women of status, including doctors, lawyers, and high-level female executives.

One day a waitress, Samantha, walked into Maria's office with a story about how her former male boss physically groped her and made a variety of sexually harassing comments to her. When she turned down her boss's invitations for sexual favors, her boss terminated her from employment. Samantha suffered from insomnia and anxiety after these events, but immediately found another waitressing job which paid even more than the previous and was performing well in that job at the time she met with Maria.

Maria evaluated the case and recognized that there were limited, if any, economic damages resulting from Samantha's claims, but there was potential for an emotional distress claim and attorney-fee recovery. Samantha, however, did not have enough income to even pay Maria's standard retainer amount, which was aimed at covering the costs of filing the complaint and other costs associated with bringing a lawsuit.

Maria, as an advocate for women, wanted to help Samantha enforce her rights to be free from sexual harassment in the workplace, but simultaneously recognized that if she took her case, it would be a lot of work with a relatively small pay out, and the time she spent on Samantha's case would detract from the time she would be able to spend on her higher profile cases with larger potential payouts.

Maria believed that she had a duty to help Samantha enforce her rights and, although Maria decided not to take Samantha's case, Maria made personal phone calls to some of her colleagues at other firms. Eventually, she found a qualified attorney who had the time and desire to take on Samantha's case and referred Samantha to that attorney. By making the time to ensure Samantha had adequate representation to enforce her rights, Maria was able to build trust with a member of the community.

While Maria acted primarily out of duty, her actions also accorded with justice because her actions protected a vulnerable party, Samantha, by helping her gain access to adequate legal representation. Justice is an amorphous concept that is embedded in the very Preamble to the U.S.

Constitution, which declares, among its noble purposes, that it is intended to "establish justice."[12] Justice involves notions of need, equality, reciprocity, desert, and fairness.[13] Ensuring justice in adversarial contexts requires making difficult decisions about ensuring justice on both micro and macro levels. Many micro-level decisions that ensure justice for one or a few people aggregate into macro-level shifts toward a just society. This magnifies the importance of striving in each case to ensure that justice is achieved. While many theories of justice are aimed at ensuring macro-level justice, such as John Rawls's veil of ignorance heuristic, the micro-level justices can be sought and attained by advocates by considering, not only legal rights but also notions of need, equality, reciprocity, desert, and fairness when making decisions. To say that justice involves these notions leaves a lot of room for discretionary acts, but such moral free space is necessary to ensure that justice is achieved and tailored to the individualized circumstances of each situation or case. Consider how Breanna tried to ensure justice for her client in the following example.

JUSTICE IS NOT ALWAYS SERVED AT THE COURTROOM TABLE

Breanna was a family law attorney who regularly appeared before the family courts in her local judicial district. She was well-known in her region, respected by her colleagues, and was very familiar with the nuances of family law in her state. However, the judicial district within which Breanna practiced recently underwent a major reassignment of judges. Pursuant to this district-wide reassignment measure, judges that had no experience in family law matters were appointed to the family courts. This created unexpected obstacles for practicing attorneys in the district because these judges did not know the law as well as attorneys like Breanna did, and often the attorneys had to educate the judges on complex family law issues.

One newly reassigned family court judge, Judge Smith, garnered a reputation for not making sound decisions that conformed to precedent and statute. He refused to learn the nuances of family law so as to effectively preside over such disputes. There were rumors that Judge Smith was insulted by his recent reassignment, and he desired a more prestigious role within the judiciary. He looked down on family matters and saw them as a waste of time. His decisions were often made on instinct, quickly, and without a full analysis of the facts and law of the case.

One of Breanna's cases was transferred to Judge Smith upon his reassignment and Judge Smith butchered the outcome of her case. From Breanna's view, and under well-known precedent, this case should have been a clear win for her client, but Judge Smith, as he became known for doing, decided instead to "split the baby," instead of abiding by precedent.

Breanna's client was disappointed in the outcome which was contrary to all expectations. Breanna attempted to explain to her client that Judge Smith was recently reassigned to the family law court and was making a lot of controversial decisions, and that if the client wanted to appeal the decision to the appellate court, or request reconsideration, that she would have a very high probability of success. Breanna shared with the client the case law that should have, but didn't, govern Judge Smith's decision, and how Breanna believed that the appellate court was the best option for overturning Judge Smith's bad decision.

Breanna's client was frustrated and upset. The client didn't fully understand how a judge couldn't follow the law. It just didn't make sense to her, and this led to her questioning Breanna's counsel, and the representations Breanna had made about the potential outcome for her case in family court, prior to Judge Smith's reassignment. In the end, the client did not wish to spend any more money on a family matter and begrudgingly resolved to accept Judge Smith's decision.

To attempt to rebuild trust with her client, and because Breanna was also frustrated by Judge Smith's decision, Breanna offered to handle the appeal on a pro bono basis, with the understanding that the client would just pay costs of the appeal (but no attorney fees). The client agreed to this arrangement, and ultimately Breanna was successful on appeal and had Judge Smith's decision overturned.

In the previous example, Breanna not only sought justice for her client, but also displayed virtuousness. The core values of advocacy are closely tied to virtue ethics. Honesty, integrity, zealousness, respect, and responsibility are often identified as virtues, but they are not an exclusive list of values an advocate should aspire toward, but other virtues including patience, kindness, compassion, courage, temperance, humility, and modesty may play a role in various advocacy contexts. In the prior example, Breanna displayed compassion for her client who faced injustice in family court. Although Breanna's solution of offering services at cost is not appropriate in all circumstances, in this situation, she felt it to be the right thing to do. The traditional mean between two extremes approach to moral virtues is one way of perceiving the balancing act of deciphering virtuous activity in each unique circumstance. Like the tuning of a guitar, when the pitch is too high, then too low, and eventually just right, eventually one can recognize the virtuous course of action. The pursuit of happiness, as described in the Declaration of Independence, is also closely tied to the virtues. As one embraces the virtues, and builds a virtuous character, one can eventually attain happiness. Consider how Kevin, in the next example, flowed with the movements of the situation to promote not only virtuous behavior but also a positive outcome for his client.

THE PRO SE LITIGANT

Kevin, an associate attorney in a general practice firm, was asked to cover a motion in court for one of his senior partners. The motion involved a relatively unique family law issue that was filed by a pro se ex-husband and father. The pro se father filed a motion requesting that he no longer be required to pay the mother child support, which the mother was using to pay part of their daughter's college tuition, and that instead he be permitted to pay the college directly for his part of the tuition and fees associated with his daughter's education. Kevin was assigned to represent the mother for this motion which was filed by the pro se father. This father had a history of not paying child support on time, which led to concerns that if the pro se father were to get what he asked for, that the parties' daughter's college tuition would go unpaid.

When the case was heard in the courtroom, the pro se father had the opportunity to make his arguments to the judge. The pro se father went on several lengthy and irrelevant tangents, talked about what was discussed in mediation, quoted hearsay, and seemed argumentative and even "slimy" to Kevin. Rather than interject with objections as the pro se litigant made many inappropriate comments and statements that violated the rules of evidence, Kevin decided to allow the pro se father to go on talking because it seemed to Kevin that the pro se father was undermining his own case. Kevin patiently waited as the pro se father continued talking for about 20 minutes until he ended his soliloquy and the judge asked Kevin for his response.

Kevin responded first by commenting that he does believe that every pro se litigant should have his day in court, although for the record, Kevin identified the many procedural errors made by the pro se father during his speech. Kevin then made a brief, argument that accorded with the law and the facts. In this situation, Kevin thought it best to be brief, to the point, and to focus on the issues. The Judge then ruled in favor of Kevin's client by denying the pro se father's motion.

By showing respect for the rights of the pro se father, not trying to "bully" the pro se father, and by being patient as the pro se father undermined his own case, Kevin was able to attain a successful outcome for his client. Had Kevin taken a more aggressive approach or not embraced the virtues of respect and patience, the outcome may very well have been different.

In the previous example, Kevin displayed virtue in his actions while simultaneously respecting the rights of pro se litigants. Lawyers seeking to build real trust should consider virtue, justice, duty, rights, and consequences when engaging with clients and all stakeholders. It is not a matter of picking one of these approaches, but instead, in a pluralistic fashion, all aspects of all theories should be considered and weighed. The normative dimension is particularly helpful to deciphering what one should be doing, but the descriptive dimension can also aid in deciphering the prevailing norms of the industry. If things are regularly done in a local court, it does not mean these things are the right thing to do, but they may be an accepted practice in that locality. Being armed with this information can provide counsel with an understanding of the landscape within which one is practicing and the accepted practical conventions. Abiding by ethical principles and social norms also has correlations with increased profit in many contexts.[14] Identifying wrongful conventions, even if accepted by a locality, and rebelling against injustices can best be explained in terms of good trust.

Good Trust

Good trust is attained through embracing moral identity. One's moral identity may be considered as "a place where individuals find a sense of their own well-being in the welfare of others."[15] Good trust is attained through pursuing moral excellence by promoting the common good and genuinely caring about others. Empathy, compassion, and concern for humans are all involved in good trust. There is an element of advocacy that involves passionately invigorating others to perceive justice or injustice through a common lens. Empathy is relevant to the attorney as a counselor who cares about what happens to a client and reveals that care and concern through words and actions. Clients are not mere dollar signs, but they are people who seek legal counsel to resolve problems that they themselves are not equipped to handle alone. Respecting clients because of their humanity is a part of ensuring the common good is achieved.

Good trust can be built with clients through emotional or communal connection which may be on intellectual, philosophical, or spiritual levels. It is the kind of trust not easily ascertainable but the kind of trust that leaves a lasting impression on a client who is able to come into the fold and feel as though they are a part of a shared community. Those who are represented become family - they laugh and cry with their counsel. There is mutual respect, concern, and appreciation shared between counsel and client. The bond grows through continued communication, understanding, and the development of a common higher purpose that transcends the individual's case into the realm of justice and principle. Adding to this transcendence is a shared understanding that the fight is for what's right and not merely over money or personal interests.

BUILDING TRUST THROUGH A SHARED HIGHER PURPOSE

Ben represented five Hispanic firemen in failure to promote lawsuits against an historically white male-dominated municipal fire station. After filing the lawsuit, in an effort to undermine the lawsuit, the fire station promoted two of the Hispanic firemen, who had the strongest cases against the fire station, yet the other three plaintiffs remained in their same positions, having repeatedly been denied promotion while lesser qualified and lesser experienced white males were promoted over them. This fire station had a long history of cronyism and favoritism. The white males who dominated the fire station did not abide by the merit-based criteria that was supposed to be used for promotional decisions, but instead promoted their friends, other white males, to positions of power and prestige.

Ben and his five clients all shared in the higher purpose of promoting equality for Hispanics in their municipality. After the two plaintiffs were promoted, they asked Ben if they should drop out of the case. Ben and the promoted clients talked and decided to continue their cases against the fire station even though their economic recoveries were now limited to minimal back-pay damages, and no front-pay damages. The primary reason the clients decided to continue their claims despite minimal recovery was that staying in the lawsuit would benefit the other three unpromoted Hispanics and all Hispanic firemen. They didn't want to allow the fire station to "sweep it under the rug."

Ben was able to foster a shared feeling of purpose among his clients based on ending the long history of discrimination in this municipality and helping future generations of Hispanic firemen from facing the same obstacles to success that the plaintiffs in this action faced. In other words, Ben and his clients were interested in institutional changes towards equal treatment, and their individual financial circumstances, while important, were only one part of a larger shared purpose.

Ben and his clients were able to embrace a shared purpose to work toward their goal of institutional change. However, those who embrace notions of common good and transcendence are often accused of being manipulative. Those who manipulate often accuse those appealing to a higher purpose of attempting to manipulate through appeals to justice or other principles. Faith in what's right, what's just, and in the goodness of others must continue to overcome such accusations. Those who care little for ethics will use it as a sword against those who they know care about ethics, by, among other strategies, playing on the guilt that good people feel when they do wrong. These are the worst kind of actors because they use goodness against those striving to be good to attempt to leverage advantage. To foster good trust with clients and other stakeholders one must be ready to overcome such pernicious behavior and to persevere through strife.

Fort describes good trust in organizational contexts as a combination of music, mediation, and more mediation. Music involves "a sense of spiritual and aesthetic, harmonic artfulness that defines a quest for moral excellence."[16] Mediation is "an organizational dimension where there are communal identities formed and which dialectically interact with individuals …. communities that foster personal meaningfulness" with moral identity.[17] More mediation "connects very concretely and specifically with a teleological goal of how corporations can contribute to sustainable peace."[18] Fort is suggesting that organizations can build trust with stakeholders by embracing higher or transcending purposes. His approach involves personal interactions that enhance a shared credo among members of a firm and its stakeholders. While sustainable peace is one such goal that Fort proffers, it may not be a realistic goal for law firms. Law firms can nonetheless share in transcending purposes, such as the protection of individual rights, promoting equality, equalizing disproportionate power relationships, or fighting for justice. The vision of a law firm can be established through shared goals that place a check on individual abuses of self-interest. Living that credo can build good trust with clients and other stakeholders.

In the following example, Nicholas and Shameka attempt to create an open environment in their law office to build trust with their employees.

THE BUSY OFFICE

Nicholas and Shameka were partners in their own general practice law firm, which had been in business for about five years. They had a staff of about a dozen employees including, associate attorneys, paralegals, legal assistants, an office manager, and a receptionist. As a small firm, they had the common problem of high employee turn-over particularly in the legal assistant positions. Nicholas and Shameka evaluated how they could improve the culture of the firm so that they could improve employee retention.

They decided to have a series of listening sessions with small groups of their employees, to give them the opportunity to discuss the turn-over issues, and to create an open space for the employees to make recommendations about how the firm could improve employee retention and culture. Nicholas and Shameka invited three employees at a time to lunch and asked them targeted questions to elicit feedback on these topics and rotated through different groups of employees in small-group settings.

What they learned was that the legal assistant positions were understaffed given the increased volume of business and that the firm needed to hire at least one more legal assistant to make the hours and workload comparable to the other employees of the firm. They also learned that the other employees often felt obligated to work through lunch and breaks to meet deadlines, and regularly felt burnt out.

Nicholas and Shameka decided to hire additional staff and continued the small group lunch meetings. When the lunch meetings were scheduled, all the other employees were encouraged to also take their lunch breaks. This reduced the perception that employees should not be taking breaks. Nicholas and Shameka rotated different employees into the lunch meetings on a regular basis, mixing up the groups, and created a continued open space for discussion of firm issues. With targeted questioning and regular small group discussions, the employees were able to open up to the partners about issues they were facing, and a safe space for voicing values was created.

Building Trust in Attorney Relationships

Fort's tripartite vision of trust provides a lens by which attorneys can devise ways of building trust with clients, court, and other stakeholders. The three types of trust do overlap, and in combination provide a framework for thinking about how trust can be fostered in legal practice contexts. Hard trust, real trust, and good trust work in combination – none alone can develop meaningful and trust-based relationships with others. It is through compliance with laws and professional rules, abidance to moral principles and societal norms, and through embracing transcendence and the common good that lasting relationships can be built. A failure in any of these dimensions can undermine an attorney's reputation, standing in the community, and prospects for success.

Many law firms have embraced business-centric models as opposed to historical models of law as a learned profession that renders service. The learned professions historically include law, medicine, ministry, and academics, but within capitalistic societies these professions which historically were aimed at putting the good of others before one's own professional gain have evolved into profit centers. To avoid the devaluation of law as a profession, those in the field must begin modeling trustworthy behaviors to those entering the profession, create a safe space wherein lawyers can discuss moral issues, provide community service opportunities, and embrace a narrative of competence that involves building trust with the stakeholders of the legal profession.[19] Lawyers have obligations to the public and to the private parties who hire them. In balancing these obligations, Fort's tripartite vision of trust can help guide practitioners to building a better profession.

In some cases, however, trust can be lost through ethical violations and attorneys must find ways to address it. The next chapter, Chapter 6, provides a sketch of a framework that subordinate attorneys can follow when their supervisors breach their trust by engaging in unethical conduct.

Notes

1   Sam Ro, Here's Why We Call It Black Friday, *Business Insider* (November 25, 2015), https://www.businessinsider.com/meaning-of-black-friday-retail-accounting-2015-11

2   Timothy L. Fort, *Business, Integrity, and Peace* 131 (2007).

3   Model Rules of Professional Conduct, American Bar Association, https://www.americanbar.org/groups/professional_responsibility/publications/model_rules_of_professional_conduct/model_rules_of_professional_conduct_table_of_contents/

4   Model Rule 1.1, American Bar Association, https://www.americanbar.org/groups/professional_responsibility/publications/model_rules_of_professional_conduct/rule_1_1_competence/

5   Model Rule 1.1, Comment on Rule 1.1, American Bar Association, https://www.americanbar.org/groups/professional_responsibility/publications/model_rules_of_professional_conduct/rule_1_1_competence/comment_on_rule_1_1/

6   Model Rule 1.3, American Bar Association, https://www.americanbar.org/groups/professional_responsibility/publications/model_rules_of_professional_conduct/rule_1_3_diligence/

7   Model Rule 1.3, Comment, American Bar Association, https://www.americanbar.org/groups/professional_responsibility/publications/model_rules_of_professional_conduct/rule_1_3_diligence/comment_on_rule_1_3/

8   Model Rule 1.5, American Bar Association, https://www.americanbar.org/groups/professional_responsibility/publications/model_rules_of_professional_conduct/rule_1_5_fees/

9 Model Rule 1.6, American Bar Association, https://www.americanbar. org/groups/professional_responsibility/publications/model_ rules_of_professional_conduct/rule_1_6_confidentiality_of_ information/

10 *Id.*

11 Keith William Diener, The Restricted Nature of the Profit Motive: Perspectives from Law, Business, and Economics, 30 *Notre Dame J.L. Ethics & Pub. Pol'y* 225 (2016).

12 U.S. Constitution, Preamble (1787).

13 See generally David Schmidtz, *Elements of Justice* (2005); and John Rawls, *A Theory of Justice* (1971).

14 Timothy L. Fort, *Business, Integrity, and Peace*, 184–188 (2007).

15 *Id.* at 199.

16 *Id.* at 200.

17 *Id.*

18 *Id.*

19 For similar recommendations for medical school education, see Jack Coulehan, Viewpoint: Today's Professionalism: Engaging the Mind But Not the Heart, 80 *Academic Medicine* 892 (October 2005).

6

THE UNETHICAL EMPLOYER AND FIRM ENVIRONMENT

Employees of firms, including associates, paralegals, and other staff, are inherently in disproportionate power relationships with their employers. The more powerful employer, which may be an attorney, owner, partner, or other manager, can control and direct the actions of subordinates. Under the Rules of Professional Conduct, those acting under the direction of an attorney must comply with the professional rules.[1] However, there are no formal mandates that require anyone to be ethical beyond mere compliance with laws and professional rules. For this reason, employees can be placed in precarious situations when their ethical inclinations do not run parallel to the dictates of their employers. The need to ensure self-preservation through income must be balanced against the (sometimes) conflicting desire to act upon values. A firm's culture plays a pivotal role in ensuring an appropriate balance for subordinate employees.

Firm Culture

Every organization has a unique culture driven by the individuals who work there and particularly those in authority positions. The ethical atmosphere

DOI: 10.4324/9780429507847-9

of a firm is largely driven by those at the top of the organization. Some refer to this as the "tone at the top," which involves a "trickle down" effect to those lower in an organization.[2] When those in charge are committed to building trust or engaging ethically with others, then that viewpoint will impact those lower in the organization, thus increasing the likelihood that they too will be committed to building trust and engaging ethically with others. The reverse is also true, the message from the top that only money matters, and not ethics, also trickles down. The unfortunate reality is that there are successful jerks in this world. One does not need to be ethical to have financial success, but financial success is better enjoyed and more sustainable when one has the trust and respect of others.

Law firm cultures span the gamut of values and compliance approaches to ethics. Compliance approaches to ethics generally take "thou shalt not" type positions within firms, focusing on what people should not do and the potential sanctions for engaging in the prohibited behavior. Ethics becomes a stick intended to motivate to comply with the rules because of fear of the consequences of noncompliance. On the other hand, firms that adhere to values approaches to ethics better position ethics as the responsibility of each member of the firm and as an integral part of the culture of the firm. Values approaches involve those at the top setting an example of genuine concern for doing the right thing beyond baseline compliance with the law and professional rules. Values approaches involve motivating with the carrot, instead of the stick, and training employees to believe in more than bottom-line profits. Compliance and values approaches, however, are not mutually exclusive.[3] Law firm cultures that embrace both values and compliance approaches in their ethical programs tend to both hold employees accountable and inspire aspirational behaviors. Consider the following example of a senior member of a law firm, and how his questionable activities affected subordinates in the firm.

TALKING THE TALK, BUT NOT WALKING THE WALK

Tony was the most senior partner of a large multi-national law firm with thousands of attorneys serving various practice groups. He was the founder of the firm's ethics institute which required all new associate attorneys to go through extensive ethics and compliance training in their first year with the firm. He was a regular lecturer at the institute which he founded decades ago and regularly spoke about the importance of integrity in legal practice at local bar association events and at firm meetings. Tony was well-respected not only for his legal acumen but also for his dedication to improving the profession and instilling values into the firm's culture. In addition to his involvement in the ethics institute, Tony also ran the law firm's litigation department, presiding over dozens of practice groups and hundreds of attorneys.

Last year, the firm hired an outside auditor to run an internal audit. It was uncovered that Tony overspent his department's budget by hundreds of thousands of dollars in the preceding two-year period. The auditing team was shocked that such an enormous amount of money could be spent unnoticed. The auditing team then identified millions of dollars of overspending in Tony's litigation department over the preceding ten years, including a variety of personal transactions made by Tony, such as the unauthorized purchase of designer clothes, box seats at sporting events, dinners at five-star restaurants, and expensive trips to exotic destinations.

Shortly after the auditing team reported its findings to the firm's management, a young associate at the firm, Colleen, reported that Tony had seduced her when she first started working at the firm five years ago, by taking her out to expensive dinners and on exotic trips. She was 24 and he was 68 at the time. She had previously been terrified to say anything about this relationship because of the power Tony had over her career, as the most senior partner in the firm. After Colleen reported Tony's conduct, dozens of other current and former women employees of the firm made similar accusations against Tony. Several civil lawsuits for sexual harassment followed and Tony was put on paid leave pending an investigation.

In subsequent media interviews, Colleen said that she regretted not coming forward sooner, and that had she done so, she could have prevented others from experiencing the type of harassment that she faced as a young female attorney. As a newcomer to the legal practice and business, she thought her career would be destroyed if she spoke out against Tony. It was her fear that prevented her from acting in accordance with her values.

In Colleen's case, she allowed fear to stop her from immediately speaking out against unethical conduct, and it wasn't until Tony was caught misappropriating funds that she was able to muster the courage to come forward. Most firms, at a minimum, embrace compliance with the law and professional rules, not necessarily because it is the right thing to do, but at least because a failure to do so could lead to negative consequences. In extreme cases, however, some firms or attorneys, such as Tony, ignore even these baseline requirements because of greed, time constraints, or other motivations. When those at the top ignore the law or professional rules, subordinate employees are placed in precarious positions. The rest of this chapter outlines factors subordinate employees should consider when working under employers who act unprofessionally or unethically and sketches a generalized framework for addressing such situations.

A Multi-step Framework for Addressing Ethical Violations of Superiors

There is no easy way to address a superior's ethical violations. One should tread carefully in any instance and proceed cautiously through multiple steps to decipher the appropriate course of action for each situation. A sketch of a framework for addressing ethical violations by superiors is outlined in Figure 6.1 and described in the following paragraphs. This framework reveals how the Giving Voice to Values (GVV) methods and strategies may be employed as a part of a broader decision-making process for addressing ethical violations of superiors. This framework should be perceived as a "sketch" or a "guideline" for decision making, and not one that is to be rigidly applied.

Figure 6.1 Guidelines for Decision Making

Conduct Risk and Cultural Assessment

The first step is to conduct a risk and cultural assessment of the firm. This assessment should involve: (1) identifying if there are any governing policies, procedures, codes of conduct, or other firm guidelines; (2) examining how the firm has historically addressed ethical issues; (3) talking to others to decipher their opinions on such matters; and (4) concluding from one's experience within the firm and knowledge of oneself how the supervisor and other stakeholders may react to the strategy you are contemplating.

If there are policies and procedures for addressing ethical issues, they should typically be followed. Well-drafted procedures will generally include a mechanism for addressing ethical issues (e.g., talk to human resources or to a supervisor). Following internal policies and procedures is paramount to ensuring one is protected if one's attempt to address ethical issues subsequently leads to retaliation. If one is working in an environment with no established procedure for addressing ethical issues or other guidelines for compliance, then the other factors involved in the assessment become even more important in determining who to approach, what to say, and how to say it.

Looking to firm history and previous ways that ethical issues were discussed or addressed is informative to deciphering the conventions of the firm. The history can be gleaned from conversations with others in the organization, review of relevant files (if any), and other institutional sources. How the firm has historically addressed ethical lapses, the seriousness of the attitude given them, and the actions taken by the firm can guide one's thinking when deciphering the appropriate strategy for addressing concerns within a specific firm.

Talking to others both within and outside of the firm about the issue and how to respond may provide insight into the appropriate strategy for addressing an ethical mishap. One could consult with other trusted employees of the firm about how they would handle the issue, if they think it significant, if they would support addressing the ethical issue, as well as any similar issues they have faced and how those issues were handled. One could also consult with outside mentors, other members of the legal field that may have experience with such issues, or even the bar ethics committees to determine one's responsibilities. Many states have hotlines that can be called for informal ethics opinions.[4] Speaking with others, both inside and outside the firm, can be an excellent source of guidance and insight.

Strategies and tactics for effectively having these conversations to effectuate change is at the heart of the *GVV* methodology. Consider the following
example of how Lydia strategically approached a colleague about her supervisor's questionable behavior.

THE AGGRESSIVE BOSS

Lydia, a newly hired paralegal, along with a few other members of her
firm, were copied on a series of emails within which her attorney supervisor, Jeremy, and opposing counsel in a million-dollar litigation were corresponding. The correspondence escalated from a simple disagreement
to a full-fledged argument. Jeremy made some very threatening and
demeaning statements to opposing counsel. When Lydia read through
these emails, she was embarrassed that Jeremy had taken things so far
and had engaged in ad hominem attacks on opposing counsel. Jeremy
was clearly the aggressor. Opposing counsel acted rationally and profes-
sionally in the face of Jeremy's attacks, insults, and spiteful messages.
Lydia at that moment felt ashamed to be Jeremy's paralegal, and desired
to voice that she thought he went overboard in his messages, but simultaneously didn't want to offend her boss or be perceived as critical.

Rather than directly addressing the issue with Jeremy, Lydia stopped by
the office of one of the other attorneys, Katie, who was also copied on the
email exchange. Lydia approached the topic in casual conversation by asking if Katie had seen the emails from Jeremy. Katie responded that she had
and before Lydia could inquire further, Katie commented that Jeremy was
really "getting out of hand," and that she'd seen Jeremy "get nasty" with
opposing counsel on several occasions over the years, but this "was particularly bad." She commented that Jeremy was developing a reputation for
being difficult to work with among local attorneys, but, at the same time,
people know he "means business." In fact, she explained that some clients
hire Jeremy because they know he'll really "stick it to" the opposition.

Lydia felt validated by Katie's comments and expressed her agreement. She then asked Katie if anyone had ever approached Jeremy about
his unique style? Katie responded that almost every other attorney in the
firm had asked him to "tone it down" at one time or another, but that
Jeremy is the "way he is" and refuses to change his style. Katie said that
she believed this situation required another conversation and offered to
join Lydia in a three-way sit-down meeting with Jeremy.

By talking with colleagues and taking an "inquisitorial" as opposed to "accusatorial" approach, Lydia was able to identify an ally who was more senior than her in the firm and was willing to join her in addressing the issue with Jeremy. By talking to Katie and learning more about the firm's culture, Lydia was able to better assess the situation and to identify a more senior ally to join her in addressing the issue in a way that did not jeopardize her position at the firm.

After being in an organization for some time, one should have an idea of the firm culture and how others may react to attempts to address ethical issues. As the example of Lydia and Jeremy illustrates, knowing the personalities and temperaments of those in the organization, and the feelings of others toward those temperaments, will help one decipher how much of a risk addressing an ethical issue would be to one's position in the firm. Whether one would be regarded as a "snitch" or a "hero" for addressing an ethical issue is largely a function of the culture of an organization, and will impact the way one frames one's approach to addressing a concern. Prior to raising an ethical issue, one should think holistically about who will be affected by the strategy one invokes, the potential consequences on one's career and personal well-being, and the potential reactions of others. The examination of these factors is key to developing an effective strategy for addressing an ethical issue.

Not only is an understanding of the organization important but so is an understanding of oneself including one's own strengths and weaknesses.[5] When addressing an ethical issue, one should appeal to one's strengths by utilizing comfortable and effective ways of communicating the issue to others. What is comfortable and effective will surely vary among individuals because personalities differ. Part of deciphering the way to address an ethical issue in organizational contexts is understanding oneself, and how to frame things in a way that one is comfortable talking to others. While the "inquisitorial" approach worked for Lydia, other people may be more comfortable with a more direct or assertive approach to addressing ethical issues. One should play to one's strengths and address issues in a way fitting oneself, others involved, and the culture of the organization.

Communicate Concerns Internally

Based on the risk and cultural assessment, the second step is to devise a strategy for communicating the concerns internally within the organization.

GVV provides a variety of strategies that can be used for internally communicating a concern within an organization. GVV is aimed at heading off ethical issues before they grow too large and formal reporting or "whistle-blowing" becomes a necessary strategy.

When communicating concerns, one should consider the: (1) hierarchical structure, (2) audience and tone of the communication, (3) content of the communication, and (4) timing of the communication. If there is a mandated procedure for addressing ethical issues in the organization, it should typically be followed. If there is not, then one should examine the risks and benefits of addressing the issue with various constituents, such as one's direct supervisor, human resources, or other colleagues or superiors in the organization. The personalities and temperaments of those involved will surely play a role in deciphering when, how, and with whom to address the issue.

The audience and tone of the communication is also something that should be considered. One does not want to appear like a troublemaker or like one is addressing the issue out of spite or for retaliatory reasons. One should also be aware of personal relationships within the firm when deciding to address an ethical issue. Some people are prone to cover for their friends, and the backlash of an improperly framed communication could lead to diminishing career prospects or bullying. The tone of the communication should fit the context, and typically not be accusatory, and be framed in a way that fits the needs of the situation, such as expressing the intention of protecting the organization and all who work for it. In some cases, informal discussions may be the better strategy, but sometimes that option is not feasible under the circumstances or was already attempted and failed. In such instances, the strategy of a formal report may be necessary to best effectuate change. Consider the example of Steve, whose supervisor engaged in dodgy behavior, and how he used a "report" to effectuate his values.

THE SUPERVISOR'S IMPLICIT INSTRUCTIONS

Steve was a recent law school graduate who was waiting on his bar exam results. While waiting for his results, Steve took a contract position with a big firm doing document review through a staffing agency. As a temporary contractor, he was given limited training composed of a one-day summary of the coding techniques to be used during this large-scale document review.

Steve was one of about a hundred temporary attorneys who was hired to review millions of electronically stored documents in a short time frame. All the temporary attorneys were housed on two floors of a large office building, with attorneys sitting in tables of four, each with their own computer. The floors were open 16 hours a day and the temporary attorneys were encouraged, but not required, to work all 16 hours. The firm had several upcoming discovery deadlines it had to meet to defend its Fortune 500 client.

The document review project was managed by several of the large firm's staff attorneys, with Brian, a senior staff attorney, leading them all. After a few days on the project, Steve noticed that the attorneys sitting at his table were not coding the documents properly. In fact, they were coding documents that were clearly relevant to the litigation as irrelevant. Because these documents were coded as irrelevant, they would not be produced in discovery. Looking over the other attorney's shoulder as he was coding, Steve noticed one document particularly, which was a "smoking gun" document, which was coded as irrelevant, and would therefore never be produced to the other party. Steve wrote down the document number of the "smoking gun" document and went to Brian's office to discuss the improper coding with him.

Steve approached Brian in a humble manner, by asking him questions about what might be relevant to the case, and then asked specifically, as a hypothetical, "what if someone found a 'smoking gun' document?" and explained hypothetically the document he saw his colleague code as irrelevant, and "if it would be relevant?" Brian responded that such a document would not only be relevant but would be "devastating to their case" and that he just hoped that "the plaintiffs' attorneys would never get their hands on a document like that."

Steve was a bit confused by Brian's response, and so queried further, "well Brian," he said, "if such a document existed, wouldn't we have the obligation to produce it to plaintiffs even if it would harm our case?" Brian responded that "we would only have to produce it if we knew it existed, and as far as I know, this document does not exist – so let's end this conversation here and both get back to work."

At this point, Brian's message to Steve was clear – that Brian did not want Steve to tell him anything further or know anything about a document that could potentially break his case. Steve acquiesced to Brian's request to end the conversation but didn't feel right about following Brian's implicit instructions. Over the next day, Steve struggled with this moral issue, and continued to feel conflicted by his supervisor's instructions which seemed to violate Steve's personal ethics and everything he'd been taught in his law school professional responsibility class. At the same time, Steve hadn't even yet passed the bar exam, and thought that maybe this is just the way things are in the "real world."

Steve, who didn't have many mentors, reached out to his law school professional responsibility professor, and asked her for advice, framing the situation as a hypothetical. With guidance from his professor, Steve recognized that Brian's instructions were contrary to not only Steve's personal moral code but also professional requirements.

After consulting his professor, Steve decided to send a formal email to Brian and the other staff attorneys identifying the "smoking gun" document by number, explaining its content, and framing it as a "report of an important document that will impact the case." Because of the overwhelming relevance of this document, rather than reporting Brian's questionable behavior, Steve framed the email as a though he was merely "reporting an important document," and that "he wanted to bring it to their attention through email because of its relevance to the case." Although Brian did not respond to Steve's email, a couple of the other staff attorneys thanked him for identifying the document and for the email.

As the preceding example of Steve illustrates, a formal report is one tactic that may be used to strategically address ethical issues. While not all reports need to be formal reports of ethical violations, there are a few "rules of thumbs" to keep in mind when formally reporting ethical issues. First, the content of the report should align with the tone and audience. Second, the report should be made in writing and the writing should be preserved in a format that will remain accessible to the reporter even after termination. Third, the report should be carefully crafted to identify what the issue is, when it occurred, who is involved, and one's rationale for why it is an ethical violation. Fourth, the report should be submitted in a timely manner, as soon as possible after the violation occurred. Fifth, typically, the report should be sent only to those who need to know and should not be publicly disseminated or first orally pronounced in a public forum like an office meeting.[6] While reporting ethical violations may be necessary in some circumstances, in instances like Steve's, a report may alternatively be used to strategically correct a potential ethical issue. The preceding "rules of thumb" should be tailored to the individual circumstances of such strategic reports.

Once the ethical issue is addressed internally, either through informal conversations, other GVV strategies, or in the most extreme cases, through a formal report, then the next step depends on how the employer responds. If the employer is receptive to addressing the issue and to correcting the wrong, then the conversation continues and becomes more about the best ways to correct the issue. If the employer is not receptive, then other strategies, such as external reporting may become necessary. This chapter next addresses how to correct an ethical issue and then, following this discussion, returns to external reporting.

Correct the Ethical Mishap

How to correct an ethical mishap will depend on many factors including: the type, scope, and severity of the violation. In all circumstances, one should effectively document what occurred, the steps one takes to remedy it, and why those steps were taken. To provide a sketch of an infraction typology, there are (1) slight infractions, which include incidents involving wrongful conduct that do not violate any laws or professional rules; (2) major infractions, which include incidents that do violate professional rules, but do not involve legal violations and/or have not yet significantly harmed others; and (3) severe infractions, which involve incidents that violate law or professional rules and (i) are legal violations and/or (ii) have significantly harmed others. While this typology will inevitably contain some gray areas, or locale or context-specific nuances, it provides a lens by which one can view various infractions. The intention of the typology is not necessarily to fit an infraction into a specific category, but rather to recognize that there are various levels of infractions, some of which involve only ethical concerns and some of which have other societal ramifications, such as legal ramifications. The typology also provides a shared language that can be used to discuss the various levels of infraction.

Slight infractions may include workplace bullying (that does not violate the law, e.g., being a jerk), making false statements that do not rise to the level of fraud, being mean or nasty to others, or a variety of other types of misconduct. Correcting a slight infraction may involve some combination of an apology, public statement, or the advent of new policies within the firm. Slight infractions should be recognized as being wrong and a message should be sent to the members of the firm that they will not be tolerated, but in most instances, slight infractions need not result in the termination of the perpetrator. The strategies used for addressing a slight infraction will inevitably vary based on the circumstances.

Consider the case of Stacey's situation as one of the few women in a male-dominated environment, and the steps the firm took to correct ongoing wrongs within the firm.

THE ROOSTER'S NEST

Stacey was one of only a few female attorneys in a mid-size law firm. While the firm had many female paralegals and legal assistants, the practice area Stacey worked in was historically male dominated with few women entering the niche field. Stacey felt she had to work longer and harder to gain the respect of her male counterparts and that she had to endure "locker room talk" and other inappropriate behavior to be accepted within the predominantly male clique that was the law firm.

The male attorneys, who were mostly young and single, would regularly go out to bars after work, to men's clubs, and would smoke cigars and drink bourbon together on the weekends. Tales of their nighttime antics were common topics of conversation during business hours, and often included stories of their womanizing exploits. These conversations made Stacey uncomfortable although she felt as though she had to tolerate them to be accepted with her male colleagues. She didn't want to be "that female attorney" who complained about the way the men were acting. Although the men would talk about inappropriate topics at work, they otherwise treated Stacey with respect.

After years of Stacey tolerating the behavior, the firm then hired a new female associate, Skylar, who was fresh out of law school and eager to make a name for herself in the field. Skylar was offended by the conversations of her male colleagues and, in fact, one of the male colleagues had dated her sister, who described him as a "player." Although Skylar wanted to succeed in the firm, she took her concerns about the locker room talk to Stacey, a more senior attorney, and expressed how inappropriate she thought it was.

Rather than addressing the guys directly and creating potential problems for Skylar's career at the firm, Stacey decided to talk to the firm's managing partner in confidence about the issue. In collaboration without an outside consultant, they developed a comprehensive code of conduct which covered everything from punctuality to appropriate office behavior, implemented the code of conduct, and required that every member engages in training, conducted by the outside consultant, on the code of conduct. The code of conduct included sanctions for violations of the code, such as the elimination of annual bonuses. The managing partner and Stacey privately told the consultant to stress the code's prohibition of "locker room" talk in the workplace, and so several exercises in training were devoted to same.

As in Stacey's case, implementation of new codes and policies, along with training may in some cases remedy infractions in the workplace. While this case may borderline on a legal violation, such as a hostile working environment, Stacey and the firm were able to take action to correct the infraction before it rose to that level (of a lawsuit).

Major infractions, such as violations of confidentiality requirements, conflicts of interest, or the mishandling of client funds may require different approaches. While any of these infractions could potentially lead to significant harm to a client, if caught early enough, they may not yet cause harm to a client, and steps could be taken to rectify the mishap before significant harm is caused to a client. In such instances, one could work with one's local disciplinary board to correct the mistake and develop new policies to ensure the infraction does not recur. The disciplinary board can assist with guiding the firm to the appropriate action either through advisory opinions, informal hotline opinions, or other forms of consultation. As is suggested by the following example, working with the board can show the firm's good faith in attempting to comply with the rules.

THE DEPOSITING DILEMMA

Frank owned his own solo practice law firm and employed a part-time paralegal and office assistant to support the management of his practice. Frank's income stream flowed primarily from a few wealthy clients although he would take on other matters as needed to sustain his business.

During a slow month, Frank took on a business matter at a "flat rate," meaning that he accepted a set $6500.00 for handling the transaction, instead of his normal hourly rate. The matter involved forming a limited liability company and writing an organizational agreement for a start-up web design company. Frank handed the $6500 check to his office assistant, Ericka, and orally instructed her to deposit it at the bank.

Usually, Frank would tell Ericka when a check needed to go into the firm's escrow account and be held in trust. However, many checks would come in from the wealthy clients who paid bills for services already rendered, and these would go into the firm's operating account. As Frank did not indicate otherwise, Ericka assumed this was a check for services already rendered and so deposited the check in the firm's operating account. However, the rules in this state required flat-rate fees to be held in escrow until project completion.

The following week, as was the standard practice, Ericka paid the firm's monthly bills from the firm's operating account and, it being a slow month, Frank did not have a surplus in his operating account. About $5000 of the $6500 deposit was used to pay bills.

A few weeks later, Frank, who had still not completed the operating agreement for the start-up web design company, noticed that the $6500 deposit was never made in his escrow account. He contacted Ericka who explained it was deposited in the operating account and used to pay last month's bills. She apologized for the mistake and was accountable for her error.

Frank, who had meticulously avoided commingling client funds with his own for his entire career, did not know what to do. He firmly believed it his responsibility to comply with professional rules, so called his local bar ethics hotline for advice on how to handle the depositing error. He was able to work with his local bar to document and correct the error.

While Frank's case involved an honest mistake, and he took immediate steps to rectify it, sometimes ethical issues arise because of deliberate acts and have severe consequences for those involved. Severe infractions may include fraud, misappropriation of client funds, overbilling, or not paying employees as agreed. When a supervisor violates law or a professional rule that significantly harms another, much more difficult decisions will need to be made about how to handle the situation. In these instances, careful thought should be given to how one frames the conversation with one's employer, as is reflected in the following example of Chris and Stephanie.

THE CON ARTIST

Chris was a local attorney with a known disciplinary history, who had a history of client complaints filed against him with the local bar association. Most of his client complaints related to mishandling client funds, fee disputes with clients, and lacking diligence in his representation of clients. Chris was able to talk his way out of most of these complaints but, in one case, the bar association did issue a public reprimand.

Stephanie, a recent law school graduate who just passed the bar exam, interviewed with Chris's firm. He seemed incredibly glamorous and charming. She was excited about starting her legal career and although she learned Chris had a questionable history, she believed he had changed and was now running a legitimate practice.

Within a few weeks of being hired, Stephanie became aware that Chris was incredibly skilled at rainmaking. He brought in many new clients with large retainer fees. Once the clients were retained, Chris would hand the cases over to Stephanie to represent the clients. From that point on, Stephanie was the primary point of contact with the clients. In discussions with many of these clients, Stephanie learned that Chris had promised them unlikely results and guaranteed them outcomes that were, in many cases, contrary to the way these cases would likely turn out under the prevailing law in her jurisdiction.

Stephanie was placed in a precarious position. The clients would often catch her off-guard by telling her the promises Chris made to them. She either had to support her boss's exaggerated, or even fraudulent claims about the likelihood of success of these cases or find another way of addressing the promises. It seemed to be a no-win situation for Stephanie whose name was on all the legal pleadings in the cases, and whom these clients were counting on for promised results.

After a couple of unexpected discussions with clients about unachievable results, Stephanie began clarifying with the clients that there were no guarantees of any results, and that Chris's conversations with the clients were based on limited information. She explained that the firm wouldn't be able to fully evaluate the client's claims until after discovery was completed.

To prevent this issue going forward, Stephanie had a talk with Chris about what the clients were saying and requested she be included in all initial consultations with clients going forward. That way, she could hear what Chris was telling them. She framed the request in Chris's interest, explaining that his unrealistic promises could lead to malpractice suits and ethics complaints against the firm, and that she didn't want the firm to have problems.

In the previous example, instead of focusing on the difficult situation Chris was placing Stephanie in, Stephanie framed her request in a way that advanced Chris's interests. By doing so, Stephanie was able to achieve the result she wanted, was included in initial interviews with clients, and stopped Chris from making unrealistic promises to clients.

Train and Implement

Regardless of the level of infraction, documentation, policy changes, and training are often utilized to remedy the situation and ensure it does not repeat. It is not enough to implement policies, but employees must be trained on those policies until they become institutionalized, and such training should include the practicing of strategies and tactics for developing scripts and action plans to effectuate change. Over time, new policies should become a part of the way the employees of the firm do business – the norms of the organization, and employees should be given a space to voice concerns over issues as they arise. Employees should be taught the relevance and importance of the policies and procedures, and be given the opportunity to practice addressing them, so that they are prepared to deal with ethical issues as they arise. An email or posting of a policy on an internal webpage is not enough to prepare employees to address ethical issues, but rather open forums for discussion that promote awareness, analysis, and action should be fostered throughout an organization. Small group meetings where new policies, procedures, and other issues can be discussed promote group cohesion.[7] Once a new policy or procedure is put in place, it may need to be refined or tweaked as unexpected issues arise from its implementation, and so an ongoing iterative process is required and continual training and discussions over time should be conducted. Training and implementation are ongoing processes. As new employees begin working with the firm they should be brought into these discussions and adequately trained.

The GVV approach to training is particularly effective. This approach not only desires to improve *Awareness* of ethical issues in an organization by educating employees on policy, and not only to promote *Analysis* of ethical issues, but also, and most important to the GVV approach, to provide and help employees to take *Action* by practicing strategies and tactics, and by developing action plans and scripts for intervening before an issue escalates too far.

GVV posits that there are many levers that may be used to develop scripts and action plans for voicing values (Table 6.1).[8]

Table 6.1 GVV Levers[9]

Lever	Central Aspects of Lever
Examining your own experiences	Examining your own experiences and learning from your experiences to better address current issues.
Seeing for positive reinforcement	Remembering not just the failed attempts at voicing values, but also the positive outcomes and learning from them.
Selecting mentors and support systems	Selecting mentors and support systems, including mentors both inside and outside the organization.
Distinguishing preferences from orders	Recognizing that not everything is a mandate, and someone saying something may just be a suggestion that opens a dialogue.
Paying attention to substance and form	Recognizing that there are appropriate contexts for and approaches to discussing values. For instance, many prefer to have meetings to discuss issues, and would rather not just be pulled aside in the hallway to talk about ethical issues.
Playing to your own strengths	Presenting the issue in a way that fits your personality. For instance, if you are a learner, approach the issue inquisitorially. If you are a debater, approach it as such.
Aligning your point of view	Aligning your point of view with your personal purpose and/or the organizational purpose.
Practicing	Practicing ways to effectively voice values by, among other things, scripting responses to potential scenarios and developing action plans.

These levers are part of the GVV approach to training. Law firms could effectively utilize GVV to help employees prepare themselves to address issues as they arise in practice, and to move beyond awareness of policies to action planning which involves learning and practicing the techniques and strategies for addressing potential violations of policies and other ethical issues.

Assess and Monitor

In conjunction with the ongoing discussions of policy implementation and action planning, the firm should take steps to assess and monitor compliance with and the effectiveness of the firm's policies. Employee surveys, regular meetings, updating of the policies, and stakeholder input can all play a role in the assessment and monitoring process. Mechanisms should be put in place to ensure that policies stay current and remain a part of the institution so that the same ethical issue will not recur. As time passes, old policies can become forgotten or outdated. Implementing a process and dialogue for revising policies and monitoring compliance is key to effectively maintaining an ethical culture, as is creating a safe place for employees to feel comfortable talking about issues as they arise and voicing the need for change over time.

Report Concerns Externally

Returning now to the unresponsive employer who is not receptive to addressing an ethical issue. When correcting the issue internally is not an option, and an employee has exhausted all possible strategies for addressing an issue internally and nothing has worked, then the employee must move on in the decision-making framework. These situations present harder cases, and often the employee should consider whether to formally report the issue externally. In weighing whether the appropriate strategy is to take one's concerns external to the firm, in legal contexts, an employee should decipher the degree of infraction and if it is an arguable case. If a slight infraction, it typically need not be reported externally. If a major infraction, reporting it externally may or may not be prudent, and one should examine whether the purported violation of the professional rules is arguably justifiable. Severe infractions are often required to be reported externally under the rules of professional conduct.

Model Rule 5.2 provides guidance regarding reporting requirements for major and severe infractions. It includes two precepts: (1) that a lawyer is still bound by the professional rules even if acting "at the direction of another person," and (2) that a subordinate lawyer does not violate the professional rules "if that lawyer acts in accordance with a supervisory lawyer's reasonable resolution of an arguable question of professional duty."[10] The comments to Model Rule 5.2 clarify that the supervisor can assume responsibility for making decisions about arguable cases of professional duty.[11] If the matter is an arguable case, then external reporting may not be necessary. If the issue is arguable and the employee has exhausted all strategies for addressing it internally, and still believes it violates the professional rules, the employee must make the difficult call of whether to report or if there is an alternative route. Consider the following example of how Juan was able to effectively address an ethics issue with his supervisor, Warren, without resorting to an external report.

THE PRESSURED CLIENT

Juan is an associate attorney who practices under the direction of his supervising partner, Warren. Juan was recently assigned to draft a Complaint on behalf of a client in a personal injury matter. Juan contacted the client, asked the client a lot of questions, and wrote the draft Complaint based on the client's answers to the questions. Once the Complaint was drafted, Juan sent it to Warren for review.

Warren reviewed the Complaint and identified that some of the facts did not fully support the cause of action pled in the Complaint. Warren instructed Juan to modify some of the facts in the Complaint to ensure that the Complaint would withstand a motion to dismiss, which he believed the defendants would surely file. Juan explained that the client said the opposite of what Warren wanted the Complaint to say, and Warren then told Juan that he better check again with the client, because his claims will be dismissed.

Juan then called the client and asked him about the modifications Warren wanted, and if these facts, as Warren described them, were accurate, and could be included in the Complaint. Juan explained that Warren thought the Complaint would be dismissed without them. The client agreed that the facts should be included in the Complaint, although the client said that he did not really believe the modified facts were true, but that he surely didn't want his case to be dismissed.

Juan felt uncomfortable after this conversation with the client and kept thinking back to his law school lessons that taught him that as an attorney, he has an obligation not to knowingly file false statements with the court. The client, after all, just told Juan that Juan was authorized to include facts in a Complaint that the client did not believe were true, and Juan's supervising attorney instructed him to do the same.

Juan decided to do some research on the personal injury issue alleged in the Complaint and wrote a brief memo to Warren which identified an alternative theory of liability that could be utilized in the client's case. This theory did not require the inclusion of any questionable facts in the Complaint. Juan then created an alternate version of the Complaint which contained the alternative theory of liability and sent the memo and revised Complaint to Warren and requested a meeting to discuss.

Warren agreed with Juan's alternative theory, and the client then approved the revised Complaint. Juan was able to bypass a major ethical issue by finding an alternative route the firm could take, without making any accusations against Warren. Juan recognized that Warren wasn't invested in lying, but that, at the time, did not perceive another option that would allow the client's case to survive dismissal. Juan was able to give Warren and the client another option, one that did not involve lying, and that option was embraced by them both

In the preceding case, had Warren insisted that Juan file a Complaint with known false facts in it, then both Warren and Juan would have violated professional rules. While Juan was able to find an alternative solution, sometimes an employee is not able to find an alternative course of action. In such instances, if all alternatives and strategies for addressing the issue internally are exhausted, one may wish to begin looking for another job and/or report externally to the local disciplinary board.

Model Rule 8.3 requires lawyers to report other lawyers who they know have violated the professional rules, but only when such a violation raises "a substantial question as to that lawyer's honesty, trustworthiness or fitness as a lawyer in other respects."[12] In such instances, the subordinate employee is in a difficult predicament because the report to the external board could lead to the reporting attorney's own loss of income and employment. Yet, Model 8.3 could be used as a final strategy before reporting or exiting a firm. For instance, subordinate attorneys could discuss their obligation to report with their supervising attorneys, and that they don't want to report, but also don't want to lose their license. These subordinate attorneys could acknowledge to their supervising attorneys that if the supervisor is suspended or even disbarred from the practice of law, the firm may shutter, and the subordinate attorneys will lose their job and means of income. Such an approach may persuade the supervising attorney to comply with the rules.

Legal Perspectives: Whistleblowing and Retaliation

While the GVV strategies are aimed at heading off issues before they rise to major problems, a basic understanding of the legal framework may influence these strategies, and sometimes whistleblowing does become necessary.

Reporting, both internally and externally, may be a form of whistleblowing and, depending on the state in which one lives, refusing to violate the professional rules may be protected activity for which anti-retaliation protections attach.[13] In states with liberal whistleblower protections, reporting a violation of a professional rule may be protected activity which would protect the whistleblower from retaliation such as discharge, suspension, or demotion. However, not all states consider reports or refusals to violate the professional rules as a form of protected activity. Subordinate employees who report violations of professional rules or refuse to violate them may not be legally protected from retaliation.

On the other hand, in most states, reporting illegal conduct is a form of protected activity, so for severe infractions, in theory at least, the reporter would often be protected from retaliation under whistleblowing laws.[14] Public policy may also protect employees that refuse to commit illegal acts under common law exceptions to employment-at-will.[15] These laws provide some protection for employees who place themselves at risk by reporting the illegal conduct of their superiors, or when they themselves refuse to violate the law.

Other laws also provide employees who report illegal activities protection from retaliation. If the illegal acts involve reports of discrimination in employment, anti-discrimination laws, such as Title VII to the Civil Rights Act of 1964 prohibit retaliation. Even further, constructive discharge is considered a form of retaliation under Title VII, and many other laws.[16] Constructive discharge has varying standards across state and federal courts. It is roughly summarized as when an employer or its agent makes the working conditions so intolerable that no reasonable person could continue working in such conditions and so an employee is forced to sever the employment relationship. Although not a formal termination, suspension, or demotion, constructive discharge can arise when an employer or firm makes someone's working life so miserable that the person's working conditions are so intolerable that no reasonable person could continue employment under such circumstances. Employers or coworkers sometimes utilize the strategy of making an employee's working life miserable after the employee reports illegal activity to try to compel the employee to resign. In such cases, there may be a constructive discharge.

Attorneys and other employees working for public employers also have protections against Constitutional violations, such as freedom of speech. 42 U.S.C. §1983 provides the federal mechanism for enforcing Constitutional and other federal rights that otherwise have no remedy under law.[17] When public officials engage in illegal activities, such as corruption, and a public employee speaks out, as a private citizen, against that public official on a matter of public concern, the public employee that speaks out may be protected from retaliation for exercising First Amendment rights to freedom of speech. Such legal protections may similarly apply to subordinate government attorneys who speak out, as private citizens, against certain unethical acts that rise to a level of public concern. The Constitution generally prohibits governmental interference with certain rights, and §1983 provides a mechanism for ensuring the government does not interfere with Constitutional rights of individuals. Some states have state law corollaries to §1983, such as the New Jersey Civil Rights Act.[18]

Beyond Legal Protections

While legal protections may provide subordinate employees with some peace of mind when it comes to reporting illegal conduct of employers, the legal protections do not come into play in all instances of reporting legal, yet unethical conduct. Anti-retaliation laws also do not protect an employee from the inherent harm caused by an employer who engages in unethical activities. If a subordinate employee is in a position under a supervisor who is engaging in unethical conduct or directing others to do so, as discussed in more detail in Chapter 8, GVV provides multiple non-exclusive strategies that the employee could implement such as buying time, gathering allies, reframing the concerns, appealing to purpose, and reducing risk.[19] Consider the strategies Heather employed to gain a better understanding of her supervisor, Susan, in the following example.

A HARSH HISTORY

Susan was an aging senior partner in a large firm. She was raised in a generation when few women went to law school and those who did had to overcome significant social resistance. She was one of the first women attorneys in her region. She sacrificed a lot to prove herself, including an opportunity to get married and have children. Susan became bitter and resented the current generation of female attorneys who were provided more liberties than she was. These young girls did not have to overcome the same barriers that she did as an early pioneer of women in the legal industry. She began referring to female attorneys who had children as "breeders," and was particularly critical of the young female associates in the office.

Susan brought a young associate, Heather, to tears one day, after a very critical and demeaning assessment of her work product during a staff meeting. Heather was embarrassed and insulted. She saw no need for Susan to critique her work so rudely in front of several other staff members, and decided she needed to have a one-on-one conversation with Susan to "clear the air," feeling that Susan had some personal issue with her. Heather then stopped by Susan's office at a time she knew Susan wasn't too busy and requested a conversation.

Rather than expressing her true feelings of being insulted, Heather began the conversation with an apology for not producing work that met Susan's expectations and inquired as to what she could do better in the future. After hearing what Susan had to say, Heather validated Susan's comments and said she would be sure to do those things going forward. After some conversation, Susan decided to take her strategy one step further, and asked Susan if there was anything she could do to avoid being called out by Susan again like that in a staff meeting. Susan seemed surprised by this question and paused for a moment before responding.

Susan then explained that as a young female attorney, she was regularly singled out, treated worse, and had to consistently prove her worth to the organization. That times have changed, but that the female attorneys still need to work harder and longer to be treated with respect by the men, and to produce a superior quality of work. It was during this conversation that Heather recognized the struggles that Susan had been through and that her motivation for calling her out in the staff meeting was not personal, but rather it was because Susan had been treated that way as a female attorney. While Heather knew that her chances of changing Susan's demeanor was unlikely, understanding the reasons why Susan was the way she was gave Heather a better lens by which to view Susan's actions and respond to them.

Attempting to better understand the supervisor's motivation for their actions may help one devise the appropriate course of action for addressing the behavior. There is nothing illegal, for instance, about being a jerk or a bully in the workplace (in most cases, absent various situations such as when doing so is because of a protected class) or even telling little white lies that do not rise to the level of fraud. Examining the motivations of one's supervisor can help one gain a better understanding of why these things are taking place and what to do about them. As in the example of Susan above, a bullying boss may act like a jerk because of her past experiences or because she does not think others will take her seriously if she is too lenient. Similarly, little white lies may be intended to prevent harm to others that may be caused by telling hurtful truths. Considering the supervisor's motivations can help one develop a strategy for addressing the unethical behavior. In many cases, the dialogue should start with the supervisor so the employee can decipher the supervisor's rationale for his or her actions. Doing so can help one to craft effective responses to unethical behavior, rather than simply excusing it.

Examining the broader context to decipher what risks one, as an employee, may have if one were to voice dissent toward the behavior of one's supervisor may also be necessary to developing a strategy for addressing unethical behavior. On one end of the spectrum is the potential that the employee could be considered a hero for striving to put an end to unethical behavior and on the other end is the potential that an employee could be terminated or branded as a snitch. There will likely be a mix of reactions by different people in the firm reaching from either end of the spectrum to many points in between. One should prepare oneself for potential fallout by building alliances with like-minded people.

Two other strategies present themselves when all else fails: accept the misbehavior and learn to live with it or exit the firm. While the GVV framework is intended to provide strategies for dealing with issues before reaching either of these points, they are both "last recourse" strategies that may be appropriate when all else fails. A mixed strategy of accepting the behavior temporarily while seeking alternative employment may be suitable in some situations. This is particularly so when one does not have enough voice in an organization to create change.

Accepting questionable behaviors may lead one down a dark path if one accepts behaviors without believing them to be appropriate under the circumstances. Too often people stay in jobs for financial reasons when those jobs are whittling away at what it means to be human. Yet, the economic realities of modern capitalistic society often require one to stay in a volatile position at least temporarily. Like a bad marriage, it is not easy to leave a job when one has bills to pay without having something better lined up. Yet, if one's sense of self-worth or conscience is at risk, one should devise an exit strategy that balances financial and personal needs.

Motivations of Employers: A Self-fulfilling Prophecy

It was once said that one "cannot simultaneously prevent and prepare for war."[20] In a similar vein, one cannot simultaneously prevent and prepare for betrayal. In relationships, work environments, and many other facets of life, preparing for betrayal can lead to the very betrayal that one is fearing will occur. By putting up walls or other protective barriers to prevent betrayal, one often creates distrust which, in turn, leads to one losing the very relationship one was afraid of losing. Like in personal relationships with a partner who is always threatening to leave out of fear of getting left, that partner's consistent threats to leave eventually create so much instability that the relationship breaks down.

Many in business who engage in unethical activities tend to believe that others are doing the same, so they take a "knock the other person down first" or "kill or be killed" approach. Individuals who try to do the right thing are often, in this way, taken advantage of by those who do not. Those who are dishonest tend to doubt the honesty of others and prepare for betrayal thereby creating a self-fulfilling prophecy rooted in reciprocal distrust. Beyond this primal fear of betrayal, other motivations of unethical behavior include money, prestige, power, control, and other fears. Understanding that some are opportunistically advantage-seeking and have such motivations is key to developing strategies that may appeal to such individuals' interests, and to effectively voice values within firm contexts.

This chapter has shown how GVV strategies and methodologies can be successfully implemented as part of a broader decision-making framework which involves examining motivations, culture, strategies, professional rules, laws, and methods of correcting and monitoring firm ethics programs. The next chapter, Chapter 7, delves deeper into how attorneys can effectively voice values within firm contexts including and beyond ensuring compliance with professional rules.

Notes

1 Model Rule 5.2 and Model Rule 5.3, American Bar Association, https://www.americanbar.org/groups/professional_responsibility/publications/model_rules_of_professional_conduct/model_rules_of_professional_conduct_table_of_contents/

2 Deloitte, Building Tone at the Top: The Role of the CEO, Board, and CCO, *Wall Street Journal*, https://deloitte.wsj.com/riskandcompliance/2014/12/15/building-tone-at-the-top-the-role-of-the-ceo-board-and-coo/

3 Gary R. Weaver and Linda Klebe Trevino, Compliance and Values Oriented Ethics Programs: Influences on Employees' Attitudes and Behaviors, 9 *Business Ethics Quarterly* 315 (1999).

4 See, e.g., Virginia State Bar, Ethics Questions and Opinions, https://www.vsb.org/site/regulation/ethics

5 Mary C. Gentile, *Giving Voice to Values: How to Speak Your Mind When You Know What's Right*, 108–134 (2010).

6 For additional suggestions, see Amy Gallo, How to Speak Up About Ethical Issues at Work, *Harvard Business Review* (June 4, 2015), https://hbr.org/2015/06/how-to-speak-up-about-ethical-issues-at-work

7 Timothy L. Fort, *Business, Integrity, and Peace*, 217–222 (2007).

8 Mary Gentile, *Ethical Leadership through Giving Voice to Values*, Coursera Course (the levers and aspects in this table are summarized with portions quoted verbatim from this course).

9 *Id.*

10 Model Rule 5.2, American Bar Association, https://www.americanbar. org/groups/professional_responsibility/publications/model_rules_of_ professional_conduct/rule_5_2_responsibilities_of_a_subordinate_ lawyer/

11 Model Rule 5.2, Comment, American Bar Association, https://www.americanbar. org/groups/professional_responsibility/publications/model_rules_of_ professional_conduct/rule_5_2_responsibilities_of_a_subordinate_lawyer/ comment_on_rule_5_2/

12 Model Rule 8.3, American Bar Association, https://www.americanbar. org/groups/professional_responsibility/publications/model_rules_of_ professional_conduct/rule_8_3_reporting_professional_misconduct/?P HPSESSID=8af86612e8bf93d1091b3aa07d72404b

13 See, e.g., *Trzaska v. L'Oreal USA, Inc.*, 865 F.3d 155, 161 (3d Cir. 2017), as amended (Aug. 22, 2017) (In New Jersey, an "employer's instruction to an employee that would result in the disregard of the employee's professional ethical standards can be the basis of a CEPA claim" under the New Jersey whistleblowing law, the Conscientious Employee Protection Act). *Cf.* Terri Martin Kirik, Retaliatory Discharge for Attorney-Employees in Private Practice: To Do, or Not to Do, the Right Thing, 33 *J. Marshall L. Rev.* 383 (2000) ("According to the Illinois Supreme Court, an attorney who takes the ethical high road by following the Rules of Professional Responsibility does not have the foundation for a claim of retaliatory discharge"); *Jacobson v. Knepper & Moga, P.C.*, 688 N.E.2d 813 (IM. App. Ct. 1997), rev'd, 706 N.E.2d 491 (Ill. 1998).

14 See, e.g., Elizabeth Brown, Keith Diener, Lucien Dhooge, Leora Eisenstadt, and Natalie Pedersen, Employment Law and Policy, Ch. 10, *in* Kevin J. Fandl (ed.), *Law and Public Policy* (2018).

15 *Id.*

16 See, e.g., Steven D. Underwood, Constructive Discharge and the Employer's State of Mind: A Practical Standard, *University of Pennsylvania Journal of Labor and Employment Law* 343 (1998).

17 42 U.S.C. § 1983 provides that

> Every person who, under color of any statute, ordinance, regulation,
> custom, or usage, of any State or Territory or the District of Columbia,
> subjects, or causes to be subjected, any citizen of the United States or
> other person within the jurisdiction thereof to the deprivation of any
> rights, privileges, or immunities secured by the Constitution and laws,
> shall be liable to the party injured in an action at law, suit in equity, or
> other proper proceeding for redress, except that in any action brought
> against a judicial officer for an act or omission taken in such officer's
> judicial capacity, injunctive relief shall not be granted unless a declara-
> tory decree was violated or declaratory relief was unavailable. For the
> purposes of this section, any Act of Congress applicable exclusively
> to the District of Columbia shall be considered to be a statute of the
> District of Columbia.

18 See N.J.S.A 10:6-1 et seq.
19 Mary C. Gentile, Vocal Values Driven Leadership, *Strategic Finance
    Magazine* (October 1, 2021), https://sfmagazine.com/post-entry/october-
    2021-vocal-values-driven-leadership/ (the strategies and descriptions in
    this table are quoted verbatim from this article).
20 See, e.g., William R. Pace, Einstein and Federalism: Yesterday and Today,
    The Federalist Debate (2005), http://www.federalist-debate.org/index.php/
    component/k2/item/415-einstein-and-federalism-yesterday-and-today
    (attributing this quote to Albert Einstein).

Part III

VALUES IN THE PRACTICE OF LAW

Part III delves deeper into ways that attorneys can effectively voice their values in legal practice by moving beyond the strict letter of the rules of professional conduct. This Part begins by examining the professional rules and how values can play a role in promoting ethical action beyond mere compliance. Next, it adapts the stakeholder concept from business ethics literature to the legal profession and discusses how the concept and theory may provide both instrumental and normative insights to practitioners. This Part then considers that law has business components that cannot be separated from people and ethics. It suggests that the social contract needs to be modified to exclude extreme profit-seeking motivations from the legal field, and that embedding virtues and values into the education, profession, and practice of law, and implementing the strategies of *Giving Voice to Values* will over time contribute to overcoming rationalizations. Part III is intended to motivate attorneys to look to and beyond the model rules when making practice decisions.

DOI: 10.4324/9780429507847-10

7

INTERPRETING THE RULES OF PROFESSIONAL CONDUCT

There are many factors that influence the behavior and interactions of attorneys. Among them are the increasingly complex number of statutes, regulations, and court rules that guide the way an attorney interacts with courts, clients, and society. The American Bar Association ("ABA") Rules of Professional Conduct ("professional rules" or "rules"), which have been adopted by most states, provide guidance to all types of attorneys including those who are inclined to do the right thing and those who are merely trying to avoid sanctions. Some form of lawyer regulation is necessary, particularly in these contemporary times of brittle morals, backlogged courts, and overworked professionals. The professional rules provide a baseline consensus as to the outermost limits of acceptable attorney conduct and give an air of legitimacy to the legal profession. Any code of professional ethics, rules, or canons comes with benefits and drawbacks – the professional rules are no different in this respect.

The professional rules have gone through various iterations and revisions over time. The ABA's 1908 Canons of Professional Ethics originally had an "uncertain legal status" that, even when adopted by bar associations, were only "quasi-authoritative" assessments of professional obligation (and were

DOI: 10.4324/9780429507847-11

not given the force of law).[1] In part, because of the questionable authoritative force and inadequate dissemination of these early ethics canons, they were replaced by the ABA's 1969 Model Code of Professional Responsibility, and eventually by the ABA Model Rules of Professional Conduct which were adopted in 1983.[2] Since then, the professional rules have been adopted by most states thereby giving them the force of law in adopting states, and have been amended multiple times.[3] The rules, however, are just the starting point for examining one's compliance, professional, and moral obligations.

Benefits and Drawbacks of the Professional Rules

The professional rules are a form of self-regulation within the legal industry. Perhaps the greatest benefit of the rules is that they contribute to improving the public perception of legitimacy of the legal profession. The baseline shared standards of the rules provide attorneys with not only guidance with select ethical queries, but also provide the general community with a method for reporting and seeking redress for violations of those standards. The ability to file a bar ethics complaint against an attorney is a form of client empowerment which ensures a check on attorney power and action. The fear of being sanctioned under the rules provides a means of deterring attorneys from violating them. The rules can also be updated and modified over time to better address changes to society, technologies, and the profession.

While boasting many benefits, the rules have limits. They offer only general guidelines, and the provisions require interpretation, and that the interpreter attempt to comply with the spirit and not merely the letter of the rules. As one commentator explained, "[r]ules are less likely to influence behavior the more they mandate conduct opposed to self-interest and then create loopholes for those intent on evasion."[4] The rules will most effectively guide the behavior of those who already want to do the right thing. Even those who desire to do the right thing have only limited guidance as no code can be fully comprehensive or predict the nuances of every specific situation that may arise. The lack of comprehensiveness is also limited by the lack of potential contexts within which the rules may apply. Although the rules can be updated and modified, doing so takes time and often the updates cannot keep up with the rapid changes to society, technologies, and the profession. Selective enforcement of the rules also creates fairness issues and the potential for targeting some attorneys over others out of political or other motivations.

Law school education about the rules provides the foundation for "issue spotting" once a law student becomes a practitioner. This helps to build awareness of ethical issues. While one is not expected to not know all the answers, one should be trained to recognize the important questions. For instance, one need not have every nuance of the conflicts of interest rules memorized for one to identify a potential conflict of interest and recognize that one must seek additional guidance from the rules or other authorities when faced with a potential conflict. Having enough knowledge to recognize an ethical issue when it presents itself is the first step to avoiding breaches of professional duties.

Similar arguments can be made for the value of legal education in business schools. Providing business students with foundational knowledge that can inform them sufficiently to recognize when a potential legal issue confronts them, so they can seek additional guidance, is an imperative part of business education. Many businesspersons do not intentionally break the law, but some that do, violate the law because they do not recognize that their actions implicate the law. For instance, one may not be fully informed of how a meaningful interactive process is required when an employee requests an accommodation for a disability, or even how broadly the word "disability" is defined under the law to often include stress, anxiety, and depression. The lack of legal knowledge in this area, may result in a manager not identifying an employee requesting an accommodation, and a subsequent lawsuit. Similarly, the foundational knowledge of the content of the rules should be repeatedly relayed to law students and attorneys so that, at a minimum, the issues can be identified when they present themselves.

Compliance: Beyond the Professional Rules

Once the ethical issue is identified, there are several steps an attorney should take before deciding upon the appropriate course of action. Reviewing the professional rules is only the first of many steps that an attorney, who is seeking to comply with the professional rules, should take. Figure 7.1 sets forth a framework that attorneys may use to determine if an action is permitted or prohibited.[5] Legal ethics is a polycentric field involving a myriad of rules, codes, guidelines, statutes, judicial decisions, ethics opinions, and other instruments of ethics that are disseminated by a variety of decentralized authorities. This framework provides a step-by-step method of navigating the complexities of professional decision making, that is, for the analysis of ethical issues in legal contexts.

Figure 7.1 Seven Steps to Decision Making

Step 1: Identify and Analyze State Rules of Professional Conduct

State rules of professional conduct are quite nuanced – sometimes significantly so. For this reason, most generalized discussions of professional ethics begin with the ABA Model Rules and sometimes, its predecessors, the ABA Code or the Canons. Despite the educational utility of approaching legal ethics from this generalized perspective, attorneys must familiarize themselves with the unique features of their state rules of professional conduct. Like the Model Penal Code and other model laws drafted by the American Law Institute ("ALI") and other organizations, the ABA model rules are not binding unless adopted by a state. Almost all states have adopted many of the model rules as their state rules of professional responsibility.[6] Attorneys must abide by their applicable state rules of professional responsibility and should familiarize themselves with how the rules are interpreted in their jurisdiction. The ABA currently maintains a database that includes the rules of every state, along with ethics opinions, decisions, guidelines, and related materials for many states.[7]

Step 2: Review the Comments, Opinions, and Decisions Relating to State Rules

The state rules of professional conduct are only the starting point for determining professional responsibilities within a jurisdiction. Almost all states provide official comments, opinions, and decisions that interpret their rules. The comments to the state rules provide a valuable resource for interpretation. Most states base their official comments upon the ABA model comments, although some states write their own comments, and yet others adopt no comments.[8] The comments to the rules are typically perceived as "guides to interpretation" that remain subordinate to the text of the rules.[9] The comments provide a valuable resource for interpreting the rules of professional conduct.

States regularly publish ethics opinions (usually of an advisory nature) and make disciplinary decisions (regarding violations of rules and appropriate sanctions).[10] The ABA Standing Committee on Ethics and Professional Responsibility also issues advisory ethics opinions.[11] Both ethics opinions and disciplinary decisions provide guidance to those who seek to understand the boundaries of permissible action and what constitutes a violation. Ethics opinions often give more on-point guidance than do disciplinary decisions, which are often very fact-specific. In some circumstances, however, there is good reason to review disciplinary decisions. These circumstances include: knowledge about how courts decide ethics issues pursuant to their review of administrative disciplinary hearings, and the related knowledge of how courts deal with these issues in a specific jurisdiction. In the disciplinary hearings, judicial opinions are often cited in argument, and the standards set forth in judicial opinions are utilized.[12] Although there are not always applicable ethics opinions, comments, or disciplinary decisions per a niche topic, if available, they should be examined to ensure professional compliance.

Step 3: Examine Statutes, Administrative Rules, and Case Law

Statutes, rules, and case law should be examined to ensure professional compliance. Federal and state statutes, rules, and case law sometimes govern or interpret certain professional issues. Some professional issues are more likely to be found in state law or federal law, and others are available in both state and federal law. Through statutes, some states promulgate prohibitions upon the unauthorized practice of law ("UPL"), which, in turn, gives rise to case law interpreting UPL statutes.[13] Federally, the Administrative Procedure Act permits an administrative agency to decide independently if that agency will allow non-attorneys to appear before federal agency tribunals.[14] States diverge as to whether they allow non-attorneys to appear before state agency tribunals.[15] There is tension between a state's authority to regulate UPL within its boundaries and the federal government's authority to regulate its administrative agencies.[16] As such, case law interpreting this tension and other aspects of UPL has arisen.[17]

In other areas, aside from UPL, case law has developed to interpret statutes, and, even if a state does not formally legislate as to an area of professionalism, often there is relevant case law. This case law arises sometimes from the lengthy history of such ethical issues as the attorney-client privilege, which can be traced historically through the centuries.[18] Other case law arises pursuant to judicial review of administrative disciplinary decisions. The ALI issued its *Restatement of the Law (3d) of the Law Governing Lawyers* which, although not binding in and of itself, is sometimes adopted by courts.[19] The evolution of the views of both state and federal courts as to professional responsibility is reflected in case law over time. Regardless of locality or jurisdiction, case law, statutes, and administrative rules are an essential component of professional guidance.

Step 4: Check for Guidelines and Other Locality-Specific Ethics Principles and Rules

Court and bar association guidelines are sometimes available to provide direction as to expectations of professionalism. Over 100 courts and bar associations have adopted guidelines for professionalism, civility, and courtesy.[20] Often these guidelines have particular application to civility in litigation. The ABA compiles a list of many guidelines and principles of professional conduct adopted by bar associations and courts.[21] In addition to the guidelines and principles, some courts also maintain local rules and rules of evidence that include professional prescriptions. Federal Rule of Evidence 502, for example, contains provisions on the attorney-client privilege, work-product doctrine, and waiver.[22] When working in a specific court, the rules of that court are required to be followed. Attorneys must check for and abide by the rules, guidelines, and principles of courts, bar associations, and other locality-specific organizations.

Step 5: Check for Other Organizational Codes and Ethics Materials

Membership in an organization often entails express or implied abidance to that organization's code of ethics. There are many voluntary organizations available for legal professionals today which maintain internal organizational codes including practice-specific organizations and general membership organizations. If an attorney is a member of an organization with an ethics code, the attorney should review the code, as well as other ethics materials pertinent to its interpretation. Depending on an attorney's membership in organizations, the attorney may be required to comply with the ethics codes and other standards of those organizations.

Step 6: Check for Employer-Specific Ethical Guidance

Some employers develop internal ethics positions on certain topics, whether in the form of mission statements, social responsibility policies, or a variety of other instruments designed to guide behavior within an organization. Government and corporate attorneys should particularly be aware of such policies, and in government, there are frequently additional rules and regulations that require compliance. At times, employers may informally provide ethics policies verbally, through emails, or via memoranda. Before proceeding with a questionable action, attorneys should speak with and receive authorization from supervisors or internal ethics counsel prior to taking such action.

Step 7: Talk to Experts and Follow Your Moral Compass

The final step in this process is to speak with experts and, based on their advice, what one finds after exploring the results of steps one through six, and one's own moral intuition, one must decide the right thing to do, and how to best act on one's values within one's organizational setting. Some state bars provide ethics hotlines that can be called for informal ethics opinions.[23] Some state bars and organizations have ethics committees that provide ethics advice.[24] Some law firms, government agencies, and other institutions have ethics departments or counsel that can be contacted for advice. In addition to the details pertaining to a specific situation, one may ask the experts about other professional duties that have recently been invoked, or that may be unique to the location, field, or any other particularity of life or practice.

Much of the preceding seven-step framework concerns professional compliance with legal and quasi-legal mandates. Yet, this framework is most effective if one strives to follow it with an eye toward adhering to the core values of the advocate, and by strategizing effective ways to address ethical issues within one's firm.

Following Your Moral Compass: Adhering to the Core Values of the Advocate When Interpreting Professional Rules and Other Authorities

The core values of an advocate include zealousness, respect, responsibility, integrity, and honesty. These and other values play an integral role in meaningfully interpreting the rules to effectuate their intent as vehicles for promoting professionalism and curbing unethical practices that may otherwise occur. These values also underlie the justification for the implementation of the rules. The rules should be read with the aim of selecting among courses of action that would best promote these and related values and virtues. In other words, when deciphering what one may do under the rules, one should aim to select the action that best promotes these values in the individualized context of the situation. The interpretation of these rules provides a measure of discretion wherein one may, in many circumstances, select among multiple available courses of action that the rules may permit. It is in this step that the action component and the Giving Voice to Values (GVV) methodologies may be most beneficially utilized by attorneys who, unlike many general businesspersons, are bound by mandatory professional rules of conduct.

The seven pillars of GVV may aid one in more effectively following one's moral compass and thereby act upon one's values within the confines and spirit of the professional rules. These pillars are insights that may assist one in enhancing one's self-understanding so as to gain the confidence to act on one's values, choosing the appropriate course of action in a given circumstance, and strategizing ways to act upon that choice. Table 7.1 outlines the seven pillars of GVV (see the following page).

The GVV pillars involve developing more self-awareness and preparing strategies for acting on one's values. Consider how the pillars are implicated in the following examples of attorneys who have technically complied with professional rules, but desire to promote values beyond the letter of the rules.

In many instances, an attorney may choose among more than one course of action and still comply with the rules. When more than one course of action is available under the rules, one should strive to engage in the course of action that best promotes the core values of the advocate and one's other personal values. At times, this may mean selecting a course of action that best promotes respect for the client in lieu of the most profitable action. For instance, the conflicts rules allow an attorney to represent a wife in a divorce whose husband is friends with another client (the "first client"),

ble 7.1 The Seven GVV Pillars[25]

llar	Central Aspects of Exploration
alues	Examining what values are, what values are at stake, which values may be shared across stakeholders, and which values may be more personalized to you as the decision maker. There are a few values that tend to be shared across cultures and peoples, yet many are determined by background, culture, and experiences.
urpose	Defining your personal and professional purpose, how your work is meaningful, what you want your work to mean, and reflecting on purpose so it can become a source of motivation for acting on values.
hoice	Examining if you believe you have a choice, and how can we make it possible to feel like we have more of a choice. This involves recognizing that all people are capable of acting on values, and often you just need to realize that there is a choice in most situations, and acting on values requires seeing the choice to act.
ormalization	Recognizing that values conflicts and ethical challenges are a part of our everyday existence. They are not merely an exception, but we engage ethical problem solving daily and should recognize that it is normal to face ethical questions, and that we should try to prevent rationalizations from stopping us from engaging in problem solving.
lf-knowledge Alignment	Introspective thinking including considering if there are ways you can feel more confident in one's ability to act on values, and by analyzing contextual factors that have historically allowed you to more easily act on values (enabling factors) or made it harder for you to act on values (disabling factors). Learning to frame the challenge in a way that best enables you to face it.
ice	Identifying the strategies and tactics for finding your own voice, and the various strategies for voicing values including asking questions, engaging in dialogue, doing research, and listening to others. This also involves looking to contextual factors such as how those you are approaching are most comfortable, what tools and information they need, how you can enhance your own comfort, the business pattern and goals, and engaging in scripting of what you will say.
asons & tionalizations	Being aware of the typical kinds of objections, pushback, and arguments that you will likely encounter when you attempt to act on your values, and ways to counter them. These include those that may stop you from acting in the first place (e.g., it's not my responsibility or it's not worth the trouble), and those that you anticipate others may say in response to you acting on your values (e.g., that's just how things are done here or it's not a big deal).

who the attorney is also representing. Yet, doing so could potentially harm the first client's case if things were to go sour. Although the rules may allow for it and taking the second client would be the more profitable course of action, doing so would not necessarily align with one's responsibilities to the first client. Each individualized circumstance requires consideration of the course of action that will best promote the advocate's values, and the appropriate action will unquestionably differ based on the circumstances and stakeholders involved. Consider how Bill addressed the preceding issue and complied with the spirit and not just the letter of the rules.

THE NON-CONFLICT

Bill was a well-known divorce attorney who had a broad client base from the local community. He represented Wynona in her divorce against her husband, John. Wynona was a long-time client and her divorce was dragged out by a highly contested custody dispute. Both parties wanted full custody of their children.

While Wynona's case was still in process, Chris was referred to Bill by a mutual friend, and Chris desired for Bill to represent him also in his divorce. During the initial consultation, Chris mentioned John's name as a potential character witness, and someone who could testify as to Chris's parenting skills. Bill proceeded to ask Chris some questions about his relationship with John and determined that they were very close friends who talked weekly. Chris was aware that John was going through a divorce but did not until that time know that Bill was Wynona's attorney. Chris really wanted Bill, who was well-known as the best divorce attorney in the area, to represent him and said, "you know, I don't really need John to be a witness in my case – there are plenty of other people I can ask."

Bill then told Chris he'd have to check the rules to determine if his relationship to John would create a conflict of interest that would prevent him from representing Chris. After Chris left Bill's office, Bill did some research and, based on his research, he determined that he could technically represent Chris if he wanted to. There was no technical conflict under the rules in his state.

However, Bill realized that if he represented his client's husband's close friend, it could create trust issues with his client. Even the possibility of John or Chris being called as a witness in the other's case would muddy the waters further. Accordingly, Bill scripted his conversation with Chris, and relayed orally and then in a letter that he had to decline representing Chris due to a "potential conflict," and offered to refer him to another local attorney.

Although the rules of his state would have allowed Bill to represent Chris and Wynona simultaneously, Bill recognized that he had a choice and in light of his relationship with Wynona, devised a strategy for communicating to Chris that there was a "potential conflict," if even not a technical one.

To consider another example of permitted attorney discretion under the rules, the rules allow an attorney to charge a reasonable fee which, depending on the jurisdiction, may include contingency arrangements of 40% of the amount the attorney recovers for a client, along with costs. In a case involving very high costs or very little work, the attorney, although permitted by the rules to recover the 40% plus costs, may alternatively opt to reduce the fee to allow the client to recover more, particularly when the settlement amount is relatively low. Doing so is not required by the rules but does promote both respect for the client and the attorney's own integrity. Having the client sign off on a fee award is a good practice that may deter the client from later making false claims against the attorney, such as denying knowledge of the amount of fees recovered. Consider the tactic Mannie used to request that her boss allow her to reduce the firm's fee to attain a settlement for her client.

PLAYING TO MOTIVATIONS

Mannie was an associate attorney in a boutique plaintiff's personal injury litigation firm. She and the opposing party recently went to mediation to attempt to resolve a relatively small case involving minor injuries to one of Mannie's clients. There was a lot of positive energy during the mediation. It seemed like settlement was likely, that is, until the defense stopped increasing their offers, and stopped at a number that, after some reflection, Mannie realized must have been the maximum authorized by the defense attorney's client. The amount was more than enough to cover Mannie's client's economic injury and to compensate her for pain and suffering. However, once her firm's 40% contingency fee was deducted from the amount offered, the client would not even be able to cover her economic damages.

Mannie had put very few hours into the case so far. The parties decided to enter into a tolling agreement and to continue negotiations prior to the filing of the Complaint or beginning any formal legal process. Mannie was convinced that the defense's offer was the best possible outcome for her client and so decided to seek authorization from her boss to consent to a reduction in the firm's fees so that the case could settle. The reduction in fees would not affect Mannie, who was a salaried employee, but would affect the firm's overall income and the amount of money her boss would make on the case. Knowing her boss's love of money, Mannie anticipated that he would push back on her proposal, so scripted and practiced what she would say before reaching out to him.

Mannie then gave her boss a call and framed the conversation in a way that he would understand, that is, she framed it in terms of the overall maximization of the firm's profits. She explained that she had some other cases in the pipeline and that by taking a fee reduction on this case that she'd only spent a few hours on, they'd get a quick settlement, a reasonable income from it, and that she'd be able to take on some additional work that could lead to even greater payouts. Although Mannie was genuinely looking out for her client's best interest, she was able to frame the conversation in such a way that led to her receiving the authorization she needed from her boss to settle the case.

In the previous example, Mannie was able to leverage her knowledge of her boss's personality to anticipate his potential reaction to a request to "help a client," so instead framed her request in terms that her boss was more likely to respond to. She was able to achieve the outcome she wanted for her client by adjusting her approach to the circumstances.

To consider yet another example of discretion within the rules, the rules by no means require empathy for a client's struggles, but one may nonetheless take a moment to reflect on each client's situation. A client provides facts which attorneys may utilize in written and oral form to persuade a judge of a certain position. In the advocacy process it is sometimes forgotten that those facts are representative of a person's life. The facts on paper are a story of someone's life and that someone has sought legal counsel to try to resolve a problem in that person's life. Often that person is in dire straits and is relying on his or her attorney's representation to resolve the issue. It may be that the person is living through a difficult time of life and is suffering from severe stress from the ongoing litigation and/or the underlying events that gave rise to it. Empathy from counsel and the counsel's ability to recognize and have compassion for what a client is going through is not a requirement of the rules but does enhance trust and respect between the advocate and client. As the following example illustrates, sometimes an attorney should consider taking a step back and reflecting on a client's situation.

TAKING A STEP BACK

Sam and Josh are partners in their own small employment law firm. They represented Darleen, an elderly woman who was terminated from her employment under suspicious circumstances, which they believed involved age discrimination. They filed a lawsuit against Darleen's former employer which hired a large law firm that is well-known in the legal community for aggressive and intimidating tactics.

The lawsuit dragged on for years and involved the defense firm "papering to death" Sam and Josh, and extensive work by Darleen whose assistance was necessary to respond accurately to the many discovery requests and motions filed in the case. In the meantime, Darleen began having health issues and was in and out of the hospital. The stress of the lawsuit was taking its toll on her, and it became hard for her to keep up with the many requests for information from Sam and Josh's firm, information which they needed to adequately fight for her rights against this aggressive big firm.

Darleen called Sam one day in tears and explained that she would soon be entering the hospital for heart surgery, and just didn't think this case was worth fighting anymore. The lawsuit was overwhelming and she just wanted to retire and focus on her health. She wanted to drop the lawsuit and give up without any compensation. Sam discussed this phone call with Josh, who was already aware that Darleen was having trouble keeping up with the case, and of her health issues. They decided to set up a conference call with Darleen to discuss options.

Prior to the conference call with Darleen, Josh gave defense counsel a call to determine if settlement was an option. The Defense had just lost their summary judgment motion, and so the case was heading to trial if it could not otherwise get resolved. In Josh's experience, most cases would either settle early, or after summary judgment was denied. Josh, without tipping his hat as to Darleen's illness, was able to reach a preliminary agreement with opposing counsel that would cover their fees and provide Darleen with adequate compensation for the wrongs against her.

When Sam and Josh had their conference call with Darleen, they were ready to present the options of settlement or trial, and Darleen quickly agreed to the amount that Josh was able to negotiate for her, and they headed towards case resolution. By recognizing the emotional state of their client and exploring options other than what their client demanded in her moment of distress, Sam and Josh were able to attain a better overall outcome for their client.

While empathy and understanding are by no means required by the rules, Sam and Josh were able to recognize that their client couldn't physically and emotionally continue the case and so moved it toward resolution. Many lawyers have "lost the notion that there is a category of non-sanctionable conduct of which we, as a profession, simply disapprove and will not accept among our own."[26] That is because lawyers often look no further than the outermost limits of the rules to determine whether they are doing the right thing. In an accessibly written article, Dennis Rendleman displays how legal ethics is a composite of social ethics, morality, religion, and law.[27] Rendleman reveals how legal ethics is a small part of a much broader social dynamic. He recalls that sanctionable conduct is not solely rooted in the professional rules, but lawyers can be sanctioned by courts and through other disciplinary procedures.[28] The shifting values of culture and society may not persevere in perpetuity but deviation from contemporaneously accepted norms of behavior may destroy an attorney's reputation even if the rules do not prohibit such actions. This is particularly true in the age of the internet. One bad online review or scandalous news article, even if not based in fact, can diminish an attorney's client base. Much like how a report during the #MeToo movement could destroy a person's reputation even if unfounded, attorneys are perpetually and sometimes unjustifiably subject to the whims of client condemnation.[29]

The implementation of values in the interpretation of codes, rules, and the application of ethical principles will contribute to their efficacy. Yet one must first have a commitment to values to implement values in interpretation – leading back to the paradoxical circle that only those who desire to do the right thing will reap the full benefits of professional rules. It is perhaps a value in and of itself to voice that rules should be interpreted with an eye toward virtuous behavior, balancing the delicate intricacies of each situation, while seeking to act with integrity, honor, and courage. Strategic inclinations of lawyers rarely coincide with such idealistic notions particularly when opposing forces in litigation contexts do not view matters as such. The end result is that if everyone is not interpreting rules with an eye toward virtue, then society does not gain the maximum net benefits of the rules.

Giving Voice to Values was initially developed for teaching ethics in business. The field of law presents unique contexts within which to exercise GVV strategies which, at times, involve judicial intervention. It is not uncommon that attorneys are not able to resolve case-related issues with opposing counsels. In such instances, the attorneys must decide whether to file a motion or otherwise seek an order from the presiding judge. Consider the following example of how Jay voiced his values to a judge, by seeking an order barring Addison from representing a non-party witness.

TAKING A STAND

Jay was a plaintiff's attorney who was representing a client against Addison, a business defense attorney whose firm was regularly hired to represent regional businesses in litigation.

During the discovery phase of the litigation, an employee of the corporation Addison was defending was identified as a key witness – although this employee was not a party to the litigation. Addison sought to also represent this non-party witness in her deposition to ensure that the company's interests were protected.

In Addison's state, it was common for defense attorneys to represent non-party witnesses in depositions who were also employees of the defendant-corporation. However, in this instance, the non-party witness had interests that were adverse to that of the corporation, and so under the rules of Addison's state, she was not permitted to represent the non-party witness if her interests were indeed adverse to that of the corporation. In other words, the non-party witness was going to give testimony that was not favorable to her employer (Addison's client). Addison nevertheless contacted the witness, interviewed her, and offered to represent her in her deposition.

When the time came to schedule the deposition, Addison informed Jay that she was representing this non-party witness for the purposes of her deposition. Under the rules, Addison's representation prevented Jay from directly communicating with the non-party witness to interview her prior to her deposition. Jay had previously been informed that this non-party witness was going to give testimony favorable to his case, and he feared that Addison's representation of this witness would unduly influence the witness into giving unfavorable testimony.

Jay fervently believed that Addison was trying to elicit improper control over the non-party witness by representing her. However, he had no way of proving that this non-party witness had interests that were adverse to Addison's client or that this non-party witness was going to give testimony favorable to his client. The only information Jay had was inadmissible hearsay evidence from his client who told him this non-party witness was going to testify against the defendant.

Jay nevertheless felt he had to take a stand because his client's case could be undermined if Addison were able to control this witness's testimony. As a result, Jay filed a motion with the Judge explaining that he had good reason to believe that Addison was representing a witness whose interests were adverse to her client's and that her representation would likely taint this witness's testimony. He asked the judge to bar Addison from representing the non-party witness.

In the preceding example, Addison was aware of the rules, but simultaneously knew that the opposing party had no way of proving she was violating them. Because it was in her interest, she proceeded to violate the rules which prohibited her from representing a non-party witness with interests adverse to her own. Jay decided to take a stand and, even without admissible evidence, filed a motion seeking judicial intervention because he believed that what Addison was doing was wrong. As the example of Jay and Addison displays, the effectiveness of professional rules is contingent on forces beyond the control of any implementing authority or governing rules committee. It depends on attorneys, the officers of the court, ensuring they abide by the rules and, when they see other lawyers violate the rules, not just idly standing by and allowing it to happen.

Societal changes also affect the efficacy of the rules. For instance, during the coronavirus pandemic many lawyers began working virtually, and it wasn't until about a year later, when most attorneys were soon returning to the office, that the ABA issued its Formal Opinion 498 to provide guidance to virtual practitioners.[30] While impossible to predict future trends or needs, the gaps in the rules often need clarification for changing circumstances, which takes time. By the time such clarifications are made, the urgency has often passed. Yet, if such urgency again arises, the opinion is in place, although may need updating to adapt to new trends.

The effectiveness of legal ethics may also be enhanced by examining how other professions address ethical queries.[31] Legal ethics cannot be viewed in a vacuum. Questions of consent, client representation, confidence, conflicts of interest, and many other ethical issues are not unique to the practice of law.[32] Much may be learned by comparator analyses of disciplinary approaches to not only the letter of the rules, but to how various disciplines motivate their constituents to embrace values and virtues in the field. Much may be learned by examining how professionals in other fields strategize to act on their values, and what tactics and techniques prove effective in other professions. Law as an adversarial vocation involves risk management to a higher plane than many other vocations. Yet, businesses in capitalistic societies are in competition, and, indeed, that competition is said to spur ingenuity and innovation. Litigation similarly involves innovation, ingenuity, and developing new strategies and tactics for effectuating values within and beyond the mandates of the rules of the legal profession.

The next chapter, Chapter 8, suggests new strategies for case and client management for legal practitioners by adapting stakeholder theory, which originated in business contexts, to the practice of law.

Notes

1 Geoffrey C. Hazard Jr. et al., *The Law of Lawyering*, Vol. 1 1–31 (4th ed. 2015).
2 *ABA, Model Rules of Professional Conduct* (About the Model Rules), https://www.americanbar.org/groups/professional_responsibility/publications/model_rules_of_professional_conduct/#:~:text=The%20ABA%20Model%20Rules%20of,Model%20Code%20of%20Professional%20Responsibility.
3 *Id.*
4 Richard L. Abel, Why Does the ABA Promulgate Ethical Rules? 59 *Tex. L. Rev.* 639, 643 (1981).
5 Some of the content in this chapter is adapted, taken, and reprinted from Keith William Diener, Navigating Paralegal Ethics: Mapping the Terrain, *Facts and Findings Magazine* (July/August 2015).
6 A.B.A., *State Adoption of the ABA Model Rules of Professional Conduct*, http://www.americanbar.org/groups/professional_responsibility/publications/model_rules_of_professional_conduct/alpha_list_state_adopting_model_rules.html
7 A.B.A., *Links to Other Legal Ethics and Professional Responsibility Pages*, http://www.americanbar.org/groups/professional_responsibility/resources/links_of_interest.html
8 A.B.A., *State Adoption of the ABA Model Rules of Professional Conduct and Comments.*

9 *Id.* at 1–4.

10 A.B.A., *Links to Other Legal Ethics and Professional Responsibility.*

11 A.B.A., *Ethics Opinions*, http://www.americanbar.org/groups/professional_responsibility/publications/ethics_opinions.html

12 *See, e.g.,* D.C. Attorney Discipline System via the District of Columbia Court of Appeals Board on Professional Responsibility, *Disciplinary Decisions*, http://www.dcbar.org/attorney-discipline/disciplinary-decisions.cfm (a perusal of the decisions reveals many examples of the board citing to legal cases).

13 Angela Schneeman, *Paralegal Ethics* 40 (2000).

14 5 U.S.C. §555(b) (2011).

15 See, e.g., Therese A. Cannon, *Ethics and Professional Responsibility for Paralegals, 82 (7th ed. 2014).*

16 *Id.* at 82–83.

17 *Id.* (citing Sperry v. Florida, 373 U.S. 379 (1963)).

18 See generally Geoffrey C. Hazard Jr., An Historical Perspective on the Lawyer-Client Privilege, 66 *Cal. L. Rev.* 1061 (1978).

19 Susan R. Martyn, The Restatement (3d) of the Law Governing Lawyers and the Courts, *The Professional Lawyer* 115 (1997); and *Restatement (Third) of Law Governing Lawyers* (1998).

20 Therese A. Cannon, *Ethics and Professional Responsibility for Paralegals*, 489 (7th ed. 2014).

21 A.B.A., *Professionalism Codes.*

22 *Fed. R. Evid*, 502 (2008).

23 A.B.A., *Links to Other Legal Ethics and Professional Responsibility.*

24 *Id.* See also e.g., Ethics & Sanctions Assistance, *NELA*, https://www.nela.org/membership/ethics/

25 Mary Gentile, *Ethical Leadership through Giving Voice to Values*, Coursera Course (the pillars and aspects in this table are summarized with portions quoted verbatim from this course).

26 Steven C. Krane, Ethics 2000: Professional Responsibility in the Twenty-First Century: Ethics 2000: What Might Have Been, 19 *N. Ill. U. L. Rev.* 323, 328 (1999).

27 Dennis Rendleman, "Morals and Ethics and Law, Oh My!" – An Historical Perspective on the ABA Model Rules of Professional Conduct, 6 *Baltic Journal of Law & Politics* 1, 6 (2013).

28 *Id.* at 12. See also David B. Wilkins, Who Should Regulate Lawyers? 105 *Harv. L. Rev.* 799, 805–809 (for an overview of different enforcement mechanisms).

29 See generally Keith William Diener and Emmanuel Small, #MeToo and Lessons in Stakeholder Responsibility, 124 *Business and Society Review* 449 (2019).

30 American Bar Association, *Formal Opinion 498: Virtual Practice* (March 10, 2021),   https://www.americanbar.org/content/dam/aba/administrative/professional_responsibility/aba-formal-opinion-498.pdf

31 Thomas Ehrlich, Common Issues of Professional Responsibility, 1 *Georgetown Journal of Legal Ethics* 3 (1987).

32 *Id.*

8

A STAKEHOLDER APPROACH
TO LEGAL PRACTICE

Stakeholder theory provides another lens by which attorneys can examine their duties to others, both within and beyond the bounds of the professional rules. A central tenet of stakeholder theory is that managers should consider stakeholder interests when making decisions. Stakeholders include, broadly speaking, all who are affected by or can affect a decision or its outcome. Stakeholder theory is primarily a theory of management and ethics but has evolved and adapted to various disciplines.[1] Stakeholder approaches are regularly utilized by business administrators and executives to manage the financial aspects of firms. This chapter suggests something further – that stakeholder theory can be adapted and utilized as a guidepost for case and client management in legal practice contexts. The stakeholder approach provides attorneys with a process for evaluating contingencies that may otherwise go unnoticed, for mitigating risk, and for minimizing uncertainty of outcomes. The stakeholder framework offers much that can be utilized by practicing attorneys as a basis for deciphering action planning within firm contexts.

DOI: 10.4324/9780429507847-12

Brief History of Stakeholder Theory

Stakeholder theory formally emerged as a theory of management in the last two decades of the twentieth century. In 1984, the same year that Orwell fictitiously foresaw a world of tyranny, corruption, and façade,[2] the stakeholder concept was formally launched as a theory of strategic management.[3] While the theory formally developed most rapidly since 1984, the stakeholder concept was utilized in various ways in the preceding centuries. In Medieval times, the concept of "stakeholder" was used primarily in the context of gambling.[4] In the mid-1900s, there were occasional references to the "stakeholder" concept.[5] In 1963, an internal memorandum from the Stanford Research Institute (now SRI International, Inc.), utilized the "stakeholder" concept, referring to "stakeholders" as the groups that management needed to be responsive to.[6] Between 1963 and 1983, many researchers began developing stakeholder-oriented theories in the context of systems theory,[7] corporate social responsibility,[8] and organization theory.[9]

In 1984, the formal development of stakeholder theory began with Freeman's seminal publication of *Strategic Management: A Stakeholder Approach.*[10] Contemporaneous to these events, legislatures across the 50 states promulgated corporate constituency statutes.[11] By the early 1990s, over half of the states created statutes that explicitly allowed, and, in at least one state required,[12] boards of directors to consider the interests of non-shareholder constituents.[13] From Freeman's landmark publication in 1984 into the new millennium, stakeholder theory rapidly evolved as academics and practitioners began embracing the duties of business to its stakeholders. Since 1984, researchers have published many articles and books on stakeholders saying a great deal about the concept, theory, and its ethical content.[14]

From Whose Perspective and Identifying Stakeholders

A stakeholder theory for legal practice must first consider the vantage point of decision making. For purposes of this analysis, the vantage shall be that of the attorney, but this framework could also be utilized by paralegals and others involved in case management. The attorney is the primary driver of cases and decisions pertaining to them so shall be the focal point of this model (accounting for the attorney's position or rank in the law firm).

As the primary decision maker for case strategy, the attorney also has the role of ensuring veracity in every stage of litigation.

Similar to how the antiquated visions of stockholder (aka, shareholder) theory had imposed an obligation of shareholder primacy on corporate executives tasked with making decisions in business, traditional theories of legal ethics regularly asserted an obligation of client primacy.[15] Client primacy asserts an obligation to put the client first in all matters and is said to arise from the lawyer's professional role as a zealous advocate for a client.[16] The strong version of the client primacy thesis requires lawyers to put the client's interests first in all things, and to assert the client's position regardless of personal beliefs.

The obligation of zealous advocacy has been around since at least the time of the 1908 promulgation of the Canons of Professional Ethics which included a prioritization of client interests.[17] Canon 15 provided that each attorney must give his

> entire devotion to the interest of the client, warm zeal in the maintenance and defense of his rights and the exertion of his utmost learning and ability, to the end that nothing be taken or be withheld from him, save by the rules of law, legally applied.[18]

The major limits to this obligation of client primacy, at this time, were that the lawyer was not permitted to violate the law, commit fraud, or to chicane. The Canon also provided that the lawyer "must obey his own conscience and not that of his client."[19] The obligation of client primacy, much like the obligation of stockholder primacy, was, even at the times of the Canons, inherently restricted by prohibitions of law, conscience, and fraud.

The strong version of the client primacy thesis, that client desires reign supreme in all matters, is little more than a myth of professional ethics. It runs parallel to the idea that businesses should maximize profits at all costs. Businessmen who adhere to the maxim that profit maximization is the only purpose of business miss entirely the nuances of stockholder theory. Similarly, attorneys that blindly attempt to justify their actions based on notions of zeal or client primacy miss the mark entirely.

Canon 32 of the 1908 Code did not endorse unrestricted client primacy but rather endorsed a very different principle. Canon 32 stated that "above all a lawyer will find his highest honor in a deserved reputation for fidelity to private trust and to public duty, as an honest man and as a patriotic and loyal citizen."[20] While client interests are important, the "highest honor" is based in giving primacy to moral considerations, which may involve giving primacy to stakeholders other than one's client. Thus, while the strong version of the client primacy thesis does not survive scrutiny, there is good reason to endorse a weaker version of the thesis. The weaker version of the client primacy thesis requires that client desires be considered, although not necessarily followed, in major case-related decision.

Even at the time of the 1908 Canons, lawyers were required to consider a variety of stakeholders, beyond the client. The 1908 Canons outline professional obligations to opposing counsel, witnesses, media, jury, the profession, clients, and other stakeholders. The Canons specify that regardless of client demands, "it is indecent to allude to the personal history or the personal peculiarities and idiosyncrasies of counsel on the other side."[21] In other words, one cannot justify ad hominem attacks on opposing counsel by appeals to one's obligation of zealous representation.

The Canons further mandate that lawyers "should never minister to the malevolence or prejudices of a client," and should treat adverse witnesses fairly.[22] Despite client demands, attorneys should be respectful of opposing parties and adverse witnesses. Canon 20 further prescribes that, regardless of client demands, involving the media in "pending or anticipated litigation" might interfere with the administration of justice and should generally be "condemned."[23]

The Canons also placed restrictions on attorney action, regardless of client desires, in relation to juries and former clients. As to the jury, Canon 23 prescribes that "All attempts to curry favor with juries by fawning, flattery or pretended solicitude for their personal conduct are unprofessional."[24] Canon 29 further requires that lawyers uphold the "honor of the profession."[25] Canon 6 prohibits conflicts of interests with current and former clients. The 1908 Canons of Ethics acted as the guiding principles for practicing attorneys until the American Bar Association approved the Model Code of Professional Responsibility, which was then replaced in 1983 by the Model Rules of Professional Conduct.[26]

The contemporary Model Rules have been adopted by most U.S. states and similarly do not endorse the strong version of the client primacy thesis. To the contrary, the Model Rules explicitly acknowledge the lawyer's obligations to many stakeholders. The Preamble to the Model Rules provides that "A lawyer, as a member of the legal profession, is a representative of clients, an officer of the legal system and a public citizen having special responsibility for the quality of justice."[27] The Preamble acknowledges the lawyer's obligations to many stakeholders including the profession, clients, the legal system, and to the public.

Beyond the Preamble, the contemporary Model Rules have modified and expanded upon the Canons to meet the changing environment of practice in the advancing age of technology and information. There continue to be professional obligations to many stakeholders as reflected in, among other rules: Rule 1.7 (obligations to current clients), Rule 1.9 (obligations to past clients), Rule 1.13 (obligations to organizations), Rule 1.18 (obligations to prospective clients), Rule 3.3 (obligations to tribunal), Rule 3.4 (obligations to opposing party and counsel), Rule 3.6 (obligations to the media), Rule 4.1 (obligations to non-clients), Rule 4.3 (obligations to unrepresented persons), Rule 5.1 (obligations to subordinates), Rule 5.2 (obligations to superiors), and Rule 8.3 (obligations to the profession). The contemporary Model Rules reflect a virtual catalogue of professional obligations to stakeholders that will, at times, trump client desires. The following example of Destiny and Oprah presents one such instance. Consider the strategies employed by Oprah to effectuate her values in face of unreasonable client demands.

THE CUSTOMER IS NOT ALWAYS RIGHT

Destiny, a local reporter, had been arguing for a long time with several local government agencies regarding their failure to provide her with access to records under her state's open public records act. She was trying to gain access to records which she needed for what she believed would be a groundbreaking article on government corruption. Despite repeated requests which complied with her state's records request procedures, the agencies refused to provide her with the records she requested.

Destiny was furious at the government agencies and its employees who were blocking her from attaining the information she requested. Destiny independently prepared and submitted a "torts claim notice" under the state's laws and notified several government employees and agencies that she intended to sue them for negligence, along with violations of the records act.

After submitting her torts claim notice, Destiny hired Oprah, a local attorney, who had extensive experience litigating public records claims. After Oprah conducted a detailed case evaluation, she identified that Destiny did not have strong claims against several of the employees and one of the state agencies that Destiny had previously threatened to sue. Oprah communicated this to Destiny, and Destiny insisted that Oprah still sue them all, and insisted she would prevail on these claims. At this point, Oprah decided to schedule a meeting with Destiny to discuss.

In that meeting, Oprah explained her decades of experience litigating records claims, and that at her age, she didn't need the money, and didn't want to waste time on cases she thought would be unsuccessful or represent clients that wouldn't take her advice. She said that she had no desire to be sued for malpractice. Oprah explained the rationale for her case evaluation and told Destiny that if she didn't agree with her case assessment, then she would gladly refer Destiny to another attorney in the area. Destiny said she would think about it and get back to her the next day.

The following day, Destiny called Oprah and said she understood and agreed, and instructed Oprah to proceed with filing the case against the parties Oprah identified. Oprah then had Destiny execute a new retainer agreement identifying explicitly the parties that would be involved, and that Destiny agreed that the other parties would not be sued.

In the previous example, Oprah was able to use her role as an experienced advocate and success in the field to persuade a client. The Model Rules create a baseline of professional obligations for practicing attorneys, but they are far from a comprehensive vision of an attorney's moral obligations. A stakeholder approach to case management requires *ad hoc* considerations of both professional and moral obligations for each major decision an attorney makes. This involves consideration of the impact of one's decision on all stakeholders, which may include, among other stakeholders, some combination of the stakeholders identified in Table 8.1 (see following page).

Table 8.1 provides a non-exclusive list of stakeholders to a civil litigation that should be tailored to the individuals involved in a specific case – individuals who have names and faces. There are a variety of other stakeholders for attorneys involved in criminal litigation including parole officers, probation officers, policemen, prosecutors, the complaining victim, and

Table 8.1 Common Stakeholders in Civil Legal Practice

Clients	Self	Employees (Paralegals, Law Firm Staff, Other Attorneys in Firm)	Administrative Agencies
Opposing Counsel	Judges	Suppliers (deposition companies, software vendors, document review companies)	Mediators
Opposing Party	Judicial Clerks	Communities	Former Clients
Opposing Law Firm (and staff)	Supporting Witnesses	Partners (owners of the firm)	Organizations
Opposing Witnesses	Adverse Witnesses	Legislatures and Governmental Bodies (including municipalities)	Profession
Families	Bar Associations	Executive Officers	Non-clients
Tribunal	Media	Prospective Clients	Jury

other government employees and representatives. Considering the impact of decisions on stakeholders has both strategic and intrinsic benefits for attorney case management.

By considering stakeholders in major decisions, an attorney may reap strategic and financial benefits. For instance, an attorney will have a more robust picture of the interests represented in a case, and how those interests may be supported or conflict with a proposed course of action. Considering the impact on and possible responses by stakeholders when making case decisions will provide a more comprehensive picture of possible consequences of an action, which will, in turn, allow the attorney to prepare for potential repercussions or consequences of a course of action. Just as an attorney should consider the possible responses by opposing counsel to a motion or argument therein, and how that adversary may respond to a given argument, to, in turn prepare to diffuse the legitimacy of that response, an attorney should similarly consider the possible impacts on stakeholders when making decisions, and how those stakeholders may respond to each potential course of action an attorney may take.

As in the example of Destiny and Oprah above, plaintiff's counsel must regularly engage in the task of deciphering who to sue in each lawsuit, that is, whether claims should be brought against a single defendant or multiple defendants. While there are strategic benefits to bringing claims against multiple defendants, including attaining direct discovery from each, or for jurisdictional purposes (e.g., avoiding complete diversity if one desires to stay out of federal court), the decision to sue any individual or entity should be taken seriously and not taken solely for purposes of gamesmanship.

Suing a person impacts that person in myriad ways, not only financial and professional, but also psychological. The ongoing strain of being a defendant in civil litigation may pervade every aspect of a person's existence and may have a negative impact on that defendant's family. The decision to sue should not be made lightly and must be balanced against the potential benefits to the case and client. There are also disadvantages to bringing a lawsuit against multiple defendants. While witnesses may feel comfortable cooperating with a lawsuit against a business entity, adding individual defendants to a lawsuit may make these witnesses less inclined to cooperate (because they are placed at greater risk). When sued, it becomes personal to those individual defendants and to their colleagues who are often witnesses. By recognizing the impact on various stakeholders in decisions such as choosing the appropriate defendant, an attorney can better strategize for successful case outcomes. The following example of Peter reveals the importance of examining the potential power and influence of stakeholders when making litigation decision.

THE CONNECTED DEFENDANT

Peter, an attorney representing an employee of a large architectural firm, was hired to sue the firm for wrongful termination. The employee wanted to name not only the firm but also Ernie as an individual defendant and allege personal liability against Ernie. Ernie was a local architect who was a senior member of the large architectural firm, a leader in the local chamber of commerce, on the board of several charitable organizations, and very politically connected with local government officials. Peter considered the ramifications of suing Ernie individually and believed it to be a bad idea.

Peter believed that the inclusion of Ernie as a defendant in the case added little value to the case. After all, if the lawsuit were successful, the architectural firm would pay out any judgment against the firm and Ernie. Peter feared that suing Ernie would create a political nightmare that could lead to harm to his client's case and long-term employment prospects. Most wouldn't care about the employee suing the firm, but Ernie had a lot of friends and connections, and could create problems for a successful outcome for the case. Ernie had a reputation for flexing his political muscles and retaliating against those who opposed him. Throwing such a "wild card" into the case, Peter believed, was not worth the limited benefits of having Ernie named as a defendant. While Peter was not afraid to stand up to those who violate the law, he was prudent enough to choose his battles wisely, and to make case decisions that would lead to the best outcomes for his client.

Prior to filing the lawsuit, Peter set up a meeting with his client, the employee, to discuss excluding Ernie as a defendant. Peter framed the conversation in terms of his client's interests and explained his thought process and how he believed his client's chances of attaining a large pay-out would be increased if they just sued the firm and not Ernie. Peter also explained that if Ernie were sued, he may retaliate against the employee by "blacklisting" him from future employment opportunities. Ultimately, the client agreed and saw how his own interests were served by not naming Ernie as a defendant.

The case of Ernie and Peter reveals the importance of examining the potential impact on stakeholders involved in a lawsuit. Stakeholder analysis is an important step in the moral reasoning process which may be used as part of a broader strategy for case management. Peter was able to identify an influential stakeholder who could affect the outcome of his client's case and persuade his client to exclude that stakeholder from the lawsuit because it was in his client's interests.

A Typology for Adapting Stakeholder Theory to Legal Case Management

While identifying the stakeholders and the impact of decisions on those stakeholders is an important component of case management, it is equally important to recognize each stakeholder's role within the adversarial system. It is to this point that stakeholder theories of business management require adaptation to remain relevant to legal case management. This is because while business involves competition and competitors are to some extent adversaries, the adversarial element is magnified in legal contexts wherein skilled advocates zealously represent client interests. For a stakeholder approach to case management to be effective one must recognize that some stakeholders are, within the context of the adversarial system, framed to be adversaries. Others are framed as allies, and yet others are neutral. While these categories are not mutually exclusive, and roles can change, attorneys who manage cases with this typology in mind may better navigate the complexities of relationships with various stakeholders. To that effect, the strategies and tactics for voicing values to various stakeholders will inevitably need to account for the stakeholder's status as friend or foe.

Ethical obligations to adversaries are an increasingly popular subject of philosophical interest. Arthur Applbaum whimsically queries into whether all lawyers are liars, and, further, provides a philosophically oriented take on moral obligations to adversaries.[28] He concludes, among other things, that the institutions and accompanying roles they create cannot provide moral justification for otherwise immoral actions. Applbaum's conclusions suggest that while the professional rules do not prohibit all immoral behaviors, attorneys should not perceive this as a license to engage in any activities not explicitly prohibited by a fair reading of such rules. For instance, the 2016 Amendments to the Model Rules provided an explicit prohibition against lawyers engaging in discrimination or harassment against someone based on gender identity, ethnicity, or marital status.[29] Model Rule 8.4(g) now defines "professional misconduct for a lawyer" as including

> conduct that the lawyer knows or reasonably should know is harassment or discrimination on the basis of race, sex, religion, national origin, ethnicity, disability, age, sexual orientation, gender identity, marital status or socioeconomic status in conduct related to the practice of law.

The absence of this provision or a state's failure to adopt it does not create a license for lawyers to discriminate when such discrimination would be immoral in society, outside of the limited context of legal practice. The absence of a prohibition in the rules does not mint moral permission to use otherwise immoral tactics or engage in otherwise immoral acts.

Adversary stakeholders are those whose interests are framed within the adversarial system as being in opposition to one's own or one's client's interests. Adversary stakeholders may include opposing counsel, the opposing party, certain witnesses, and the team that works on the opposing party's case. While in the context of the rules of the adversarial system, these stakeholders are adversaries, it should be acknowledged that many civil claims are resolved by settlement prior to trial and many criminal charges are resolved by plea bargains. Litigation may be perceived as a mechanism for aligning the interests of the disputants so that they can reach settlement or a bargain. Prior to the effectuation of such an agreement one should proceed with caution when engaging with adversary stakeholders. However, such as in the following example of Mark and Evan, adversaries may sometimes be turned into long-term allies.

THE COLLEGIAL APPROACH

Mark was a very senior litigation partner with a large firm that had recently been retained to defend a medical facility in a malpractice case. The attorney representing the plaintiff, Evan, was only a couple years out of law school and was still learning the ropes of complex litigation. Mark knew that Evan had a strong case, and that Evan's experience was likely the weakest component of his case. Mark believed that mediating the case and keeping the case out of the eye of the public was in his client's best interest.

Although they were adversaries, Mark took on a "collegiality" strategy with Evan. Mark had long conversations with Evan and spoke about his early days in practice, some of the cases he worked on, his experience working with some of the attorneys in the area, and his work with the local bar association. He encouraged Evan to get involved with the association.

Instead of engaging as an adversary, Mark befriended Evan and developed a good rapport with him. Then, Mark offered to mediate the case, an offer which Evan gladly accepted. At mediation, the case settled for an amount that was fair to both clients. While Mark and Evan were adversaries, they were able to develop a rapport, based in Mark's collegial approach, that produced an outcome that was satisfactory to everyone involved, and ultimately attained Mark's goal of resolving the case through confidential mediation mechanisms, and out of the scrutinizing public eye.

As the example of Mark and Evan illustrates, sometimes adversaries can turn into allies. While Mark's motivations for befriending Evan may not have been fully pure, Mark was acting in what he believed to be the best interest of his client. He simultaneously provided a fair solution for Evan and his client, and the two attorneys were able to develop a collegial relationship and resolved the case in a way that benefited everyone involved.

Allied stakeholders are those whose interests are framed within the adversary system as being in alignment with one's own or one's client's interests. Allied stakeholders may include one's client, certain witnesses, and other team members who work together in support of the client's case. While in the context of the adversary system, these stakeholders are framed to be allies, the interests of allies, at times, do diverge. One such instance is when a client is unwilling to accept a settlement amount that an attorney believes is a fair deal. Other instances include billing disputes or personality conflicts. Allies have a shared interest in ensuring a successful outcome to the claims or defenses and must work together to overcome diverging interests. This shared interest may be used as an effective strategy of overcoming disputes with allied stakeholders. Consider the following example of Mawena who embraced shared interest to resolve an issue with her client, Carl.

OVERCOMING CLIENT CONFLICTS

Mawena represented Carl in a complex divorce. After over a year of contentious litigation, Carl and his wife finally were able to reach a verbal agreement that would resolve the issues of the divorce. However, divorce settlements were required to be in writing to be enforceable in this state. Carl knew this, and so relied on his wife's representations that they had an agreement and asked Mawena to write up the settlement agreement. Mawena proceeded to write the agreement exactly as Carl instructed and sent a copy to the opposing counsel for review.

Several days later, opposing counsel responded that everything in the settlement agreement was approved by his client except that she wanted an extra $10,000 over what Carl had previously agreed to, claiming that she needed it to pay off some of her student loans. When Mawena presented Carl with the counteroffer, Carl was infuriated. He began screaming at Mawena saying that his wife was trying to "take him to the cleaners" and that "this is not what we agreed to." Carl told Mawena to "reject the offer," and to take the case to trial. He said he was not going to let his wife get away with these slimy tactics.

Mawena told Carl to "sleep on it" and that they would talk tomorrow, and that she would contact opposing counsel after they talked. In the meantime, Mawena created a detailed breakdown of the marital assets and debts, and a cost projection for trial. Her calculations revealed that if Carl accepted the counteroffer, that he would likely walk away from his divorce with between $30,000 and $50,000 more in the bank than if he were to proceed to trial, taking into account costs associated with trial, and explained that the range was due to select uncertain outcomes regarding the distribution of marital property.

When Mawena and Carl talked the next day, she presented him with her financial projections and relayed to him that she agreed that his wife was being slimy, but asserted that if she wasn't slimy, they probably wouldn't be getting divorced. Mawena reminded Carl that her responsibility as his counsel was to get him the best outcome possible, and that she knew Carl's goal was also to walk away from the divorce with the best outcome possible. They both shared the interest of resolving the case in the best way possible for Carl. Mawena was able to help her client recognize this shared value, let go of his vengeful thoughts and anger, and ultimately reach a settlement.

While Mawena did not agree with Carl's reaction, she was able to use waiting, gathering information, and a shared purpose to attain the outcome she thought was right, which was to get the best possible result for her client. While some attorneys may have jumped at the opportunity to increase their income by taking Carl's case to trial, Mawena was able to effectuate her values by implementing these strategies.

Neutral stakeholders are those who, within the context of the adversary system, do not have a direct interest in supporting a particular outcome to the dispute. Neutral stakeholders may include judges, juries, mediators, arbitrators, and certain witnesses. The identification of which witnesses are adversary, allied, or neutral stakeholders is a key component of case strategy. While some witnesses may be mixed, many tend to fall into one of these three categories. Other neutral stakeholders play an important role in ensuring fairness and justice are achieved through the adversarial process. A skilled advocate may effectively turn neutral stakeholders, such as judges and juries, into allies. Consider the following example of the strategy used by George during the voir dire process. This strategy illustrates that values may be relayed to juries in a variety of ways.

EVERY MOMENT COUNTS

George was an experienced litigator who was soon starting trial. He recognized that a trial started, not at oral argument, but the moment the jury laid eyes on him and his client. He recognized that the jury was assessing both him and his client through the jury selection process.

George opted to take a non-adversarial approach to voir dire and, after one very necessary strike of a potential juror, he passed on any opportunities to strike additional jurors, none of whom were particularly reprehensible.

In the meantime, opposing counsel removed six jurors from the jury pool. George appeared professional and passed his opportunities to strike with an air of confidence and a peaceful tone. As the morning dragged on, some of the potential jurors appeared frustrated by his opposing counsel's continuous complaints and opposing counsel's dragging out of the jury selection process. Some jurors perceived this as though opposing counsel had something to hide, while George and his client did not.

While there is no doubt that jury composition influences the outcome, George recognized that the perceptions of those jurors also held power. By approaching jury selection in a non-confrontational way, George began building allies with the jurors before the trial even began by implicitly voicing his values of calmness, confidence, and non-confrontation to the jury.

The recognition of stakeholder interests, the role of a stakeholder within the context of the adversarial system, and how each stakeholder is impacted by decisions does mitigate uncertainty and aid in developing case strategy.

A Stakeholder Approach to Client Management

Stakeholder analysis can also aid attorneys who counsel clients outside of litigation contexts. The role of the attorney as an advisor extends far beyond misconceptions of the appropriate role of the attorney as that of a "hired gun" who eats nails and doesn't take any bull. Attorneys are regularly tasked with identifying options, weighing them, and evaluating the advantages and disadvantages of each course of action. The potential consequences of various options can be fleshed out by evaluating the impact of each option upon stakeholders and considering how each stakeholder may react. Stakeholders may react negatively if they are harmed by an action which may, in turn, create negative consequences for the client.

The Model Rules are consistent with a stakeholder approach to client management. Rule 2.1 provides that

> In representing a client, a lawyer shall exercise independent professional judgment and render candid advice. In rendering advice, a lawyer may refer not only to law but to other considerations such as moral, economic, social and political factors, that may be relevant to the client's situation.

The role of the lawyer as an advisor explicitly entails consideration of non-legal factors in the provision of advice to clients. These factors may include the impact of one's decision on stakeholders, conflicts of stakeholder interests, and strategies for overcoming stakeholder concerns.[30]

Clients are regularly examining new ways of cutting costs, and legal services outsourcing ("LSO") may provide a means for shaving some pennies off the expensive price tag of a law firm. Consider a business client who seeks counsel from her attorney regarding the pros and cons of LSO. To properly advise this client, an attorney should examine the impact of outsourcing on the various stakeholders and develop strategies for addressing them. Lacity, Willcocks, and Burgess provide exactly such a stakeholder approach to counseling clients who are engaging for the first time in LSO.[31] Their study concluded that "[p]roponents of the LSO relationship are the stakeholders who will 'gain' the most benefits from it, such as GCs [general counsels] held responsible for corporate spend."[32] They determined that executives and unit heads were used to outsourcing in other areas so were mostly supportive of LSO, yet in-house counsels and external law firms were resistant to the idea of outsourcing, and particularly resistant to outsourcing legal work that is more specialized.[33]

Acknowledging that in-house counsels are particularly resistant to the idea of LSO, the authors provided strategies for overcoming this resistance. These strategies include keeping in-house counsel involved, proving the concept to in-house counsel, utilizing key performance indicators, and arranging for the LSO and in-house counsel to meet face-to-face. The authors identified these strategies from working with firms and suggested them as a means of overcoming in-house counsel's resistance to LSO. If the authors had not first identified the stakeholders and determined that these barriers exist, they would not have identified the need to identify strategies for overcoming the barriers. The strategies identified by the authors, such as "proving the concept" and "face-to-face" meetings, may similarly be utilized to voice values in appropriate contexts.

Other client management situations may similarly require attorneys to identify the potential or even perceived benefits and harms to various stakeholders. The process for deciding which strategy to adopt involves: (1) making a list of all viable courses of action, (2) making a list of stakeholders for each viable course of action, and (3) identifying how each course of action may benefit or harm each stakeholder. For each course of action, Table 8.2 may be used to outline the harms and benefits to different stakeholders.

Table 8.2 Identification of Harms and Benefits to Stakeholders per Course of Action

Stakeholder (or Stakeholder Set)	Benefits	Harms
The Client		
Employees of the Client		
Friends of the Client		

By placing the names of each stakeholder or set in the appropriate column and then the benefits and harms to each, one has a more complete picture of the possible repercussions of a given course of action. One may manage for risk and mitigate against uncertainty by fully exploring the potential impact of each course of action on stakeholders. Once the harms and benefits are identified, attorneys may develop strategies for their clients that mitigate harm and overcome the barriers presented by this analysis.

The Giving Voice to Values (GVV) methodologies take hold to develop communication techniques and tactics for strategic implementation of the right course of action. Gentile provides a variety of strategies that may be utilized to effectuate values. Some key strategies are summarized on the following page in Table 8.3.

The list of strategies contained in Table 8.3 is not intended to be a comprehensive list and the strategies identified should not be viewed as mutually exclusive. To the contrary, voicing values often require the implementation of multiple concurrent strategies, or attempting multiple strategies before one works. Voicing values is a fluid process that moves with the actions and reactions of the stakeholders involved. The below example of Ben displays how one may flow with the responses of the stakeholders and use multiple strategies to achieve one's goal (see example on page 163).

Table 8.3 Strategies for Implementing Values[34]

Strategy	Description
Speak up now or later	Sometimes we're able to act or speak effectively immediately in the moment when we recognize a values challenge, but even if we miss that opportunity, we can often return to the issue later when we've had the chance to think through our response.
Buy time	If we can't effectively address an issue as it arises, then sometimes we can request more data, input, or consideration to buy time to find an effective way to address the challenge.
Address the issue	Sometimes we can point out the values conflict directly, but other times we can find ways to address the issue without embarrassing or shaming the other person. Simply offering an alternative approach allows the individual to shift gears while saving face.
Support others	If we witness someone raising a values issue, then it can be very powerful if we offer that person support publicly and/or privately.
Identify and enlist allies	If we see a challenge, then there are likely others who feel the same way. We may not know who they are, however, if we don't try to raise the issue. We can often make our points more effectively if we enlist well-chosen allies who bring experience, knowledge, and influence.
Think short-and-long term	When raising values concerns, try to raise both short- and long-term benefits of doing the right thing, as well as both short- and long-term costs of doing the wrong thing.
Reframe the concern in positive terms	If we're trying to encourage others to work with us on a values concern, then it can be helpful to frame the request as "taking a leadership role" or "building a stronger, more successful organization." Avoid framing concerns as a complaint or an accusation.
Identify and reduce risks	If we identify what's motivating all parties and what's at risk or at stake for everyone involved, then we can sometimes find ways to raise our concerns that will help people feel less vulnerable and solve their problems in a way that's consistent with the organization's values and our own.
Appeal to purpose	Support our ethical positions by focusing on the purpose and goals that we share with the individuals whom we're trying to influence, as opposed to focusing only on our differences or playing the blame game.
Counter lowest-common-denominator assumptions	Often, assuming the worst of those around us makes us think that it may be impossible to act on our values effectively, but we can create a virtuous circle by appealing to the good in our colleagues.

THE NEWBIE

Ben recently joined a small firm as a paralegal. While pursuing his paralegal degree, he minored in environmental studies. Since he graduated and joined the firm, he maintained an interest in the environment. He would regularly read articles about how to reduce the carbon footprint of businesses. He would also occasionally attend fundraisers and donate money to environmental charities.

Ben was surprised at the amount of waste the firm produced. The firm did pay for a paper shredding and recycling service, but aside from that, all plastics, glass, and cardboard were disposed of through the trash, and were not recycled. As a proponent of the environment, Ben wanted to talk to his bosses about getting a recycling bin for the firm, but he didn't want to seem like he was overstepping as a new employee of the firm. Who was he, he thought, to tell a bunch of busy attorneys that they should be recycling? He was afraid to interrupt their work and decided that he would let it go for the moment and focus on his onboarding and proving himself a valuable member of the team.

As the months went by, Ben had some successes with the firm and began to feel more comfortable with the attorneys and other staff. Ben decided to approach the recycling issue by asking one of the attorneys about it. At the end of an unrelated meeting, Ben asked the attorney, "by the way, do you know why the firm doesn't have a recycling bin?" The attorney responded that "I never really thought about it." Ben took this response as an opportunity to inquire further, and asked "would you mind if I picked up a recycling bin and put it in the kitchen?" The attorney said that "he didn't have a problem with it" but that Ben should check with Jacob (the firm's owner) first.

Ben waited another few days and when he had the opportunity to have a private conversation with Jacob, Ben asked the same question, "do you know why the firm doesn't have a recycling bin?" Jacob responded that he had "looked into it years ago" but that there was "no recycling pick up in the area." Ben responded, "okay, makes sense." Ben didn't want to preach to Jacob, and thought something should be done, but didn't have enough information to respond to Jacob at that time.

After some thought, Ben realized that if Jacob had examined the possibility of recycling in the past that it was probably something he'd be willing to do, so Ben researched options in the area. He found a recycling center not too far from his home and learned that the center accepts drop-offs 24 hours a day. With this information, Ben was ready to propose a plan to Jacob.

At his next meeting with Jacob, Ben asked Jacob if he would mind if he put a recycling bin in the firm's kitchen and said that he found a center nearby that he could drop the recycling bin off at when it fills up. As expected, Jacob said "that's fine." Ben's recycling program was launched!

Ben, as a recently hired paralegal, was hesitant to immediately approach the "busy attorneys" with his values issues. He instead employed the strategy of "speak later." When it was the right time for Ben to speak, he was careful not to shame anyone when choosing to "address the issue." When Ben didn't have complete information, he decided to "buy time" to research the issue more and develop a proposal. Having identified that he had potential allies in Jacob and another attorney in the firm, Ben garnered the confidence to effectively voice his values. Although it was not an immediate change, Ben was ultimately able to employ multiple strategies to accomplish his goal.

Differing Stakeholder Maps

Visual representations of stakeholder maps have evolved from traditional hub and spoke models to more detailed models. There are a variety of ways that stakeholders may be represented in relation to a firm.[35] Figure 8.1 (see following page) is the traditional hub and spoke model. It includes the firm in the center of the graphic, with arrows flowing in both directions between the firm and its stakeholders. The arrows flowing in both directions represent the obligations the firm owes to its stakeholders, and the reciprocal responsibilities that stakeholders have to the firm.

The regime model, sometimes called the network model, emphasizes that all members of a "regime of responsibility," have obligations to each other. A regime of responsibility (aka, a regime) is the network of interconnected individuals with shared norms or practices that are working to "get things done."[36] It is not merely a bilateral arrangement, but there exists a web of relationships, each carrying certain responsibilities to others within the regime. Figure 8.2 (see p. 166) reflects the regime model, with the

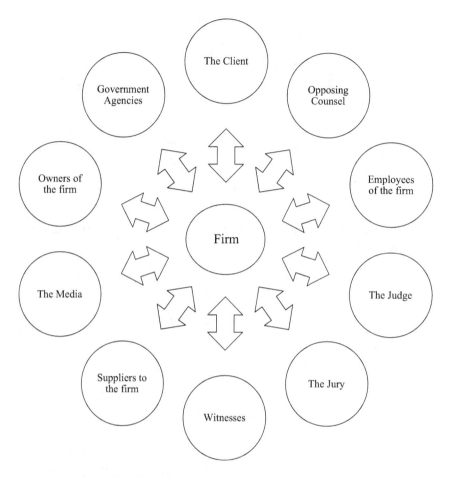

Figure 8.1 Traditional Hub and Spoke Model

arrows among regime members reflecting the obligations owed to each other. This model decenters the firm to place it within the broader construct of business and society.

Each model has benefits. While the regime model more accurately portrays the interconnected obligations among the regime members, it is a more complex model to compose and maintain. The addition of one new stakeholder requires substantial modification to the model. Making and modifying the regime model can be difficult to do with contemporary standard software programs. The traditional hub and spoke model is

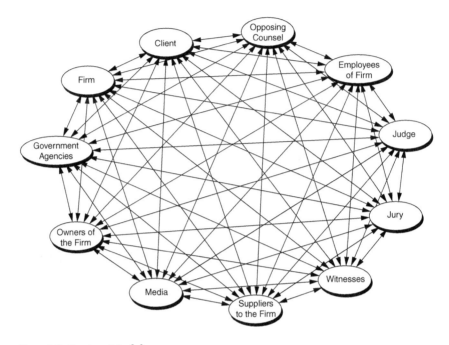

Figure 8.2 Regime Model

simpler and can easily be modified and updated to add or delete stakeholders. It can be easily composed and modified using contemporary standard
software. It is useful, at times, to have a visual representation of one's stakeholders to utilize for the purposes of conducting analyses of their interests
as cases progress. One could easily compose and print out a stakeholder
map and leave it on one's desk or in a case file as a reminder of all who are
involved in a case.

Responsibilities of Stakeholders

As the regime model illustrates, all participants in the legal system have
responsibilities not only to the firm, but also to each other. While this
chapter has focused mostly on those obligations of attorneys to their stakeholders, the stakeholders also have responsibilities to attorneys and other
members of the regime. This segment provides illustrative examples of
the responsibilities of stakeholders, and how those responsibilities may be
levers that can be pulled to effectively voice values.

Clients have a responsibility to be truthful not only to the court or when under oath, but also in all communications with their representing counsel. Many attorneys have clients who do not provide honest or complete information. These circumstances can lead to difficult queries for those attorneys who make strategic case decisions based on false or incomplete information. While prudence requires evidence before such strategic decisions are made, statements are not always verifiable. When attorneys are faced with clients who breach their responsibility of honesty, it can lead to a breakdown of the attorney-client relationship and undermine the potential for a positive case outcome. Consider the following example of how Lino used Harvey's breach of his responsibility of honesty as a lever.

UTILIZING CLIENT RESPONSIBILITIES AS A STRATEGY FOR CHANGE

Harvey worked for a large marketing firm and was recently laid off shortly after he requested medical leave. The company claimed that the layoff was part of a reorganization and had no relationship to Harvey's request for medical leave. Harvey retained Lino, who was a very skilled employment attorney who had experience litigating cases for wrongful termination and violation of family leave laws. Harvey provided Lino with the documentation of his medical leave request, his doctor's certification, some performance reviews, and the letter terminating him less than two weeks after he requested medical leave. Harvey also painted a picture for Lino of how everything changed the moment he requested leave, and the company's history of hostility toward employees who requested time off. Lino agreed to take the case on contingency, filed the complaint, and discovery began.

During discovery, some emails between Harvey and his friends were produced by the defendants and these emails clearly stated that Harvey believed he was going to be fired, and that his entire department was facing layoffs. There were several emails from Harvey discussing the then-upcoming reorganization and that he believed his job was at risk. These emails were sent in the weeks and even months preceding Harvey's request for medical leave. They undercut Lino's theory and the picture

Harvey painted about how Harvey was retaliated against and terminated for taking medical leave.

Lino called the client in for a meeting and addressed the emails and how they have undercut the chances of a successful outcome to the case. Lino explained that Harvey's failure to tell him about these emails and his advance knowledge of the reorganization has now put him in a difficult position and that the case would likely now be dismissed at summary judgment. Lino recommended Harvey agree to a very low settlement offer to resolve the case. Lino tried to phrase his language carefully so as not to call Harvey a "liar," but, indeed, the shoe did fit in this instance. Harvey agreed to the proposed low settlement offer and understood that he had breached his responsibilities to his attorney by not being forthright about his termination.

In the previous example, Lino was able to utilize his client's failure to fulfill his responsibilities as a lever for maneuvering the case in another direction which would, if successful, mitigate the harm that his client's untruthfulness caused to Lino. Lino was able to strategically use Harvey's violations of his responsibility of honesty to his attorney to convince Harvey to resolve the case.

Beyond clients, opposing counsels also have responsibilities. At a minimum, opposing counsels have responsibilities to be civil and professional. It is not uncommon for opposing counsels to violate this responsibility. The adversarial nature of legal practice combined with high stakes and client pressures sometimes combine to cause a breakdown in civil communication between opposing counsels. Some attorneys even tactically leverage animosity under the guise of seemingly advantaging their clients. Other attorneys simply fall on the opportunistic end of the bell curve and tend to act in their own self-interest in most situations without regard to values. These attorneys may fuel the volatility between opposing parties to increase their own workload and thereby their billable hours. Consider how Duane tactically addressed opposing counsel's breach of his responsibilities in the example on the next page.

In the example, Duane was able to use Fred's improper tactics against him to curb Fred's abuses of the litigation process and show how Fred was not

UTILIZING OPPOSING COUNSEL'S RESPONSIBILITIES AS A STRATEGY FOR CHANGE

Duane was a defense attorney who regularly defended large companies against tort and other claims. He would regularly defend against very vigorous plaintiffs' attorneys who would send voluminous discovery requests intended to make defending the claims against his client as difficult as possible. Fred, a plaintiff's attorney, was known in the community for being overly zealous and would often sue several defendants at once and send detailed and comprehensive discovery requests to each defendant. He would also file many motions to attempt to wear down the defendants and force a settlement.

Fred was representing the plaintiff in a high stakes tort action against Duane who represented his business client along with five of its employees. Fred proceeded in accordance with his reputation and began "papering to death" the defendants by filing motion after motion and sending discovery request after discovery request. While Duane knew of Fred's reputation, and had defended cases before, Fred's actions in this particular case went overboard, even for Fred. Fred obviously filed motions that could have been negotiated, without even attempting conversations, and Fred sent hundreds of individual discovery requests to each of the six defendants.

Duane attempted to discuss things rationally with Fred and asked him to work with him on limiting some of the requests and to communicate with him prior to filing motions to try to work things out, but Fred responded that "this is how things are done," and continued to send more and more papers to Duane without communicating with him.

Duane realized that there was no getting through to Fred, and that judicial intervention would be needed so Duane began including in all his responses and filings with the court repeated statements that plaintiff was filing this "solely for the purpose of needlessly driving up costs" and then gave examples of all the improper things Fred was doing. Duane continued to document every example of how Fred was "needlessly driving up costs" in response to each improper request sent and each motion filed. Duane was able to use Fred's breach of his responsibilities to engage in civil and professional practice to eventually put enough fear in Fred that he began attempting to resolve issues through conversation and negotiation before engaging in needless motions practice.

fulfilling his responsibilities to court and opposing counsel. In the end, Duane was able to strategically ensure that Fred complied with generally accepted norms and values. Beyond opposing counsels, managing attorneys also have responsibilities, including the responsibility of ensuring that employees of the firm abide by the rules of professional responsibility. When managing attorneys violate this responsibility, or themselves do not set a moral "tone at the top" of the firm, the lack of ethics often trickles down to the other employees of the firm. An amoral or even immoral managing attorney makes it particularly difficult for junior members of a firm to fulfill their professional responsibilities. Consider how Jackie, in the following example, used her managing attorney's responsibilities to leverage change.

UTILIZING A MANAGING ATTORNEY'S RESPONSIBILITIES AS A STRATEGY FOR CHANGE

Jackie was an associate attorney who worked directly under Lars, a solo practitioner who was hungry for business. Jackie was told that her job was to "bill hours" and was regularly told to spend a large amount of time reviewing documents in detail which really did not require much time to review. While Jackie understood that Lars had to make a living and had substantial overhead costs, including her salary, sometimes she thought that Lars took things too far and skirted the line of ethics.

After a failed pre-suit mediation, Lars instructed Jackie to file a legal Complaint against the defendant who refused to settle the case at mediation. This defendant argued that the claims Lars alleged were "frivolous," and so offered nothing at mediation. Jackie researched the issue and concluded that the defendant's analysis of the claims was correct and if the complaint were filed, it would be dismissed. She researched alternative theories but after extensive research, she concluded that there were no other viable claims. She even found a similar case which was filed and dismissed as "frivolous" by a well-respected trial court judge in the state. She brought this information to Lars's attention, but he was upset because the defendant refused to settle and instructed her to "file it anyways."

Jackie did not want to file the case and felt that if she did, she may be subject to sanctions. Prior to filing, Jackie carefully crafted an email documenting her findings and noting her concerns with filing a frivolous suit. She also reminded Lars that as her supervising attorney that if this suit were deemed frivolous, that he would also be liable even if her name were on it, and that she didn't want him or her to run into issues with the state's ethics board. She framed the email in such a way that it seemed like she was trying to protect herself and Lars from the inevitable fall out of filing a frivolous complaint. By reminding him of his responsibilities under the professional rules, and that he could be sanctioned for her filing this complaint, Jackie was able to successfully convince Lars that the Complaint shouldn't be filed.

While no two situations are the same and strategies will inevitably differ, a thorough analysis does reveal a virtual catalogue of responsibilities of stakeholders to the firm, the attorney, and other stakeholders. The examination of these responsibilities and particularly the fulfillment or violation of these responsibilities plays an important role in attorney decision making. Appealing to these responsibilities, and the potential consequences of breaching responsibilities, as Jackie did in the preceding example, may be utilized as strategies for effectively voicing values in legal contexts.

Underpinning Value Judgments of a Stakeholder Approach to Legal Practice

Value judgments play an integral role in the application of stakeholder analysis in legal contexts. Some value judgments underlying a stakeholder framework for legal practice include:

- Attorneys have moral obligations to stakeholders beyond those embedded in the rules of professional conduct. While the rules set forth an attorney's professional obligations, and there is overlap with moral obligations, the rules are not the end-all be-all of decision making in legal contexts.
- Client obligations should not always be given primacy, but rather strategies should be determined on an ad hoc basis after consideration of all professional and moral obligations to all legitimate stakeholders (including clients).

- One has moral obligations to one's adversaries. The adversary relationship is created by a system, has limited life, and is governed by the rules, not only of the profession, but by the moral rules of general society.

To act upon these value propositions, attorneys may conduct stakeholder analysis to decipher appropriate courses of action. Doing so will provide strategic and intrinsic benefits to attorneys, firms, and ultimately the clients they represent. Once the stakeholders are identified and the potential courses of action are recognized, the tenets of GivingVoice toValues take hold to move beyond awareness and analysis, and toward action planning within firm contexts.

The next chapter, Chapter 9, examines how social contract theory may be utilized to effectuate values and overcome common rationalizations in the legal field.

Notes

1 See, e.g., Leif Skiftenes Flak and Jeremy Rose, Stakeholder Governance: Adapting Stakeholder Theory to E Government, 16 *Communications of the Association for Information Systems* 642 (2005); and Fiona Cownie, *Stakeholders in the Law School* (2010) (a collection of essays examining stakeholders of law schools); and Anthony Bradney, Stakeholders in the University Law School: A Note in Dissent, *in Stakeholders in the Law School*, 225–246 (Fiona Cownie ed., 2010) (examining some of the difficulties of applying the stakeholder concept in other settings, particularly law school and university settings).
2 George Orwell, 1984 (1949).
3 Edward Freeman, *Strategic Management: A Stakeholder Approach* (1984).
4 Samuel F. Mansell, *Capitalism, Corporations and the Social Contract: A Critique of Stakeholder Theory*, 25–27 (2013).
5 *Id.*
6 Freeman et al., *Stakeholder Theory: The State of the Art*, 30–31 (2010); Freeman, *Strategic Management: A Stakeholder Approach*, 31 (1984).
7 Freeman et al., *Stakeholder Theory: The State of the Art*, 30–45 (2010).
8 *Id.*
9 *Id.*

10 Freeman, *Strategic Management: A Stakeholder Approach* (1984).

11 Anant K. Sundaram and Andrew C. Inkpen, The Corporate Objective Revisited, 15 *Organizational Science* 350, 353 (2004).

12 Margaret M. Blair, *Ownership and Control: Rethinking Corporate Governance for the Twenty-First Century*, 218 (1995).

13 *Id.*; See also Timothy Fort, The Corporation as Mediating Institution: An Efficacious Synthesis of Stakeholder Theory and Corporate Constituency Statutes, 73 *Notre Dame Law Review* 173 (1997); and Timothy Fort, Corporate Constituency Statutes: A Dialectical Interpretation, 15 *The Journal of Law and Commerce* 257 (1995–1996).

14 See Max B. E. Clarkson, *The Corporation and Its Stakeholders: Classic and Contemporary Readings* (1998); R. Edward Freeman and Robert Phillips, *Stakeholders* (2010); Robert A. Phillips, *Stakeholder Theory: Impact and Prospects* (2011); and Freeman et al., *Stakeholder Theory: The State of the Art* (2010).

15 Keith William Diener, The Restricted Nature of the Profit Motive: Perspectives from Law, Business, and Economics, 30 *Notre Dame Journal of Law, Ethics, and Public Policy* 225 (2016).

16 Tara Radin, The Professional Responsibilities of Lawyers: A Stakeholder Approach, *in Crisis and Opportunity in the Professions*, Vol. 6, 67–83, 68–71 (Moses L. Pava and Patrick Primeaux eds., 2005).

17 Canons of Prof'l Ethics Canon 15 (Am. Bar Ass'n 1908).

18 Canons of Prof'l Ethics Canon 15 (AM. BAR ASS'N 1908) (internal quotation omitted).

19 Canons of Prof'l Ethics Canon 15 (Am. Bar Ass'n 1908).

20 Canons of Prof'l Ethics Canon 32 (Am. Bar Ass'n 1908).

21 Canons of Prof'l Ethics Canon 17 (Am. Bar Ass'n 1908).

22 Canons of Prof'l Ethics Canon 18 (Am. Bar Ass'n 1908).

23 Canons of Prof'l Ethics Canon 20 (Am. Bar Ass'n 1908).

24 Canons of Prof'l Ethics Canon 23 (Am. Bar Ass'n 1908).

25 Canons of Prof'l Ethics Canon 29 (Am. Bar Ass'n 1908).

26 Tara Radin, The Professional Responsibilities of Lawyers: A Stakeholder Approach, *in Crisis and Opportunity in the Professions*, Vol. 6, 67–83, 69 (Moses L. Pava and Patrick Primeaux eds., 2005).

27 Model Rules of Prof'l Conduct, Preamble & Scope (Am. Bar Ass'n 1983).

28 Arthur Isak Applbaum, *Ethics for Adversaries: The Morality of Roles in Public and Professional Life* (1999).

29 Kristine A. Kubes, Cara D. Davis, and Mary E. Schwind, *The Evolution of Model Rule 8.4 (g): Working to Eliminate Bias, Discrimination, and Harassment in the Practice of Law* (Am. Bar Ass'n 2019), https://www.americanbar.org/groups/construction_industry/publications/under_construction/2019/spring2019/model_rule_8_4/

30 See also Michael C. Ross, *Ethics & Integrity in Law & Business: Avoiding "Club Fed"*, 117–130 (2011) (providing example scenarios that reveal how a lawyer's role is often more than a mere legal advisor).

31 Mary Lacity, Leslie Willcocks, and Andrew Burgess, *The Rise of Legal Services Outsourcing: Risk and Opportunity*, 61–64 (2014).

32 *Id.* at 62.

33 *Id.*

34 Mary C. Gentile, Vocal Values Driven Leadership, *Strategic Finance Magazine* (October 1, 2021), https://sfmagazine.com/post-entry/october-2021-vocal-values-driven-leadership/ (the strategies and descriptions in this table are quoted verbatim from this article).

35 See, e.g., Patricia Werhane, Globalization, Mental Models and Decentering Stakeholder Approaches, *in Stakeholder Theory: Impact and Prospects*, 111–129 (Robert Phillips ed., 2011). See also Tara J. Radin, From Imagination to Realization: A Legal Foundation for Stakeholder Theory, *in Re-Imagining Business Ethics: Meaningful Solutions for a Global Economy*, Vol. 4, 31–49, 34 (2002) (for a rendition of the network model of stakeholder mapping).

36 Jerry D. Goodstein and Andrew C. Wicks, Corporate and Stakeholder Responsibility: Making Business Ethics a Two-way Conversation, 17 *Business Ethics Quarterly* 375, 380 (2007).

9

THE BUSINESS OF LAW AND COMMON RATIONALIZATIONS

Law firms and its stakeholders are embedded within a broader societal construct that many theorists refer to as the "social contract." With roots in political theory, the social contract incorporates notions of not only politics, but also law, religion, science, business, and morality. The social contract may be viewed as a meta-theoretical approach that encapsulates a pluralism of other ethical theories, practices, and norms. The tradition of the social contract is one based in the consent of the people and has historically been used as a vehicle for social reform.[1] At a minimum, social contract theory may be used as a heuristic for conceptualizing the obligations and behaviors of legal professionals within society. This chapter suggests that the common rationalization of many attorneys that law is a business, and so decisions should be based solely upon financial considerations is violative of the contemporary social contract in the United States. Yet one cannot ignore that contemporary legal practice is dependent on economics, so we are tasked with reconciling the attorney's need for financial stability with the attorney's broader obligations to the members of society and its institutions.

DOI: 10.4324/9780429507847-13

The Social Contract Tradition

The social contract tradition is a manifestation of Western political thought. Its roots are in Plato's Crito, wherein Socrates examines whether he has an obligation to comply with unjust laws. As a formalized theory, Hobbes, Locke, Rousseau, and others developed their own views of the social contract beginning with a pre-governmental "state of nature" to decipher, among other things, the type and purpose of government, the nature of humans, and the obligations of citizens.[2] John Locke's influence on the founding fathers of the United States is widely accepted.[3] Thomas Jefferson himself maintained a portrait of Locke in his Monticello Estate.[4] The infamous words of the Declaration of Independence, asserting man's rights to "Life, Liberty, and the pursuit of Happiness" are largely Lockean ideas, perhaps with some Aristotelian influence, which were again manifested with the quintessential Lockean focus on "property" in the Fifth and Fourteenth Amendments to the U.S. Constitution. These Amendments prevent the government from infringing on one's life, liberty, or property without due process of law.[5]

The social contract, sometimes referred to as the "social compact," was mentioned in many early U.S. state constitutions and other legal documents such as the Virginia Declaration of Rights.[6] Over time, the concept of the social contract has been used by many to attempt to define obligations in a variety of settings including healthcare, science, and business. Most approaches to utilizing the social contract to explain professional obligations involve a delineation of the quid pro quo, or the exchange of duties, benefits, or rights between societies and the professionals or persons at issue.

The essence of the legal profession's social contract is that society grants lawyers respect, status, the privilege of self-regulation, autonomy, and financial rewards in exchange for expected competent, professional, and ethical representation of the interests of private citizens and the public.[7] Both parties to the contract must fulfill their requisite obligations for the contract to continue to make sense for the other members of society. When attorneys recurrently fail in their professional or ethical obligations, they, in turn, lose the respect society has promised them, status, and often they miss out on long-term financial rewards. Recurrent violations of the contract may result in further losses of autonomy and increases in external regulation. As such, it is in each attorney's interest to fulfill the obligations under the social contract to reap the benefits that society can offer.

When attorneys lose sight of their role as representatives of private and public rights and view the role of the firm solely as a profit-center, the contract may more easily be violated. The esteem offered to officers of the court is downgraded with stigmas akin to used-car salespersons or "ambulance chasers." The common rationalization by attorneys that justify malfeasance is that of the "business decision" which attempts to separate ethics and human beings from business. Freeman refers to this misconception as the "separation fallacy."[8] That is, people, business, ethics, and profits cannot be boxed out from each other but are inextricably linked. The common rationalization for immoral action of it being a "business decision" does not hold much weight because those decisions affect people which, in turn, affect the long-term profitability of the business. Treating employees badly or failing to follow through on agreements with opposing counsel impacts an attorney's reputation and, in the long term, will likely result in negative financial repercussions for that attorney.

It is imperative, therefore, that attorneys see past the common rationalization of the "business decision." One way of moving beyond this misconception is to consider that at the core of the legal field's social contract is the expectation that attorneys act with professionalism. Along with medicine, academics, and the ministry, the legal field is historically considered a "learned profession" aimed at serving the public and others over and above one's own interests. That is, putting the well-being of others before the professional's personal gain is at the heart of the profession of law. However, as the following example illustrates, one must first be able to recognize internal rationalizations when they occur in order to overcome them.

BUSINESS DECISIONS

Jamie was an attorney who was contacted by a potential client, Scott. Scott had little money and a case that would surely take a lot of time and effort. Jamie had a very busy practice and taking on a case for so little money and which would take so much time seemed like a bad business decision. Simultaneously, Jamie felt in her gut like Scott was truly wronged and that he had a winning case, and she knew Scott would have trouble finding an attorney in her niche practice area that would represent him for so little.

Jamie had also been taken advantage of for her good heart in the past, when she tried to help the wrong people, and was hesitant to get entangled in a similar situation again. Her first instinct was to refer Scott to another attorney, knowing full well that Scott would not be able to afford anyone in her niche practice area. Jamie began to think that this "wasn't her responsibility" and that this was a "business decision." Although she sympathized with Scott, and believed his rights were clearly violated, her first impulse was to pawn him off on someone else and focus on her more lucrative cases.

In Jamie's gut she knew she should take Scott's case and help him, but she began to rationalize away her responsibility as a professional. If not for her ability to recognize that she was indeed rationalizing, surely she would have sent Scott away with little chance of him ever finding an attorney who would help him.

Jamie began to recognize the internal rationalizations and to remember that although money is a necessity, it should not drive all her decisions. Here, she felt good about Scott, about a successful outcome for his case, and began to overcome her rationalizations by remembering she is a member of a profession which is intended to serve the public. She ultimately decided to take his case for minimal remuneration relative to her other cases because she believed in her responsibility to protect the legitimate rights of others.

In the previous example involving Jamie and Scott, Jamie began to allow her own internal rationalizations to sway her from acting on her values. By recognizing that she was rationalizing and remembering her responsibilities to the public, she was able to overcome the "business decision" rationalization and do what she believed was right.

Corresponding to the notion of a "business decision" is the intertwined rationalization that "everybody else is doing it," or the less extreme version of "others do it too." Some attorneys profit from under-handed tactics such as overbilling clients, taking questionable cases by paying clients, or acting as a "hired gun" who threatens and demeans the other party. Human beings are diverse and there will always be a segment of the legal field that engages in such tactics. Yet the legal profession (as a whole) has the power to limit and socially sanction those who engage in unprofessional or immoral behavior.

Gentile discusses how most humans fall on a bell curve. On one end of the bell are the "opportunists" who tend to act in their self-interest.[9] On the other end of the bell are the "idealists" who tend to act according to their values. Gentile suggests that most people fall somewhere on the curve of the bell, and strive to act in accordance with their values (unless it puts them at a systematic disadvantage).[10] Giving Voice to Values (GVV) is aimed at giving those on the bell curve the tools they need to be more confident in acting on their values.[11] Social sanctioning is one such strategy for motivating or even coercing those who act solely in self-interest (and contrary to values) into aligning their values with socially acceptable practices. While this strategy will not work in all instances, particularly those involving pure opportunists, it can, in the proper circumstances, prevent such opportunists from harming too many others. Consider the following example of how Carter and his colleagues were able to effectively prevent Kyle from taking advantage of others in their community.

SOCIAL SANCTIONS

The workers' compensation community in Carter's region is a very small community of practitioners. The same attorneys regularly appear before the same judges, and often have multiple cases against each other at any given point in time. Over the years, the attorneys have developed respect for the skill sets of their opposing counsels and in some cases, they are able to work together to reach resolution and in others the clients require they litigate the cases in the local workers compensation courts.

While most in the community practiced with relative integrity and were able to work together, a former personal injury attorney, Kyle, who was well known for taking questionable cases and clients, began taking workers' compensation cases and litigating them vigorously within the workers compensation courts. He engaged in underhanded tactics, such as making verbal agreements with opposing counsel and then modifying those agreements at the last minute to try to get more for his client. When opposing counsel questioned him about changing his oral agreement, he would often respond that "you do it too" and that "nothing is final until in writing."

As time went on, Kyle's reputation in the workers' compensation community became better known. Many of the other attorneys in the region knew he could not be relied on to keep agreements necessary to settle cases. So, when Carter had his first case against Kyle, Carter made some inquiries with the local members of the workers' compensation community and determined that Kyle could not be trusted. Carter therefore refused to accept any oral offers made by Kyle to settle the matter, knowing that Kyle would likely not follow through on those offers. During the case, Kyle engaged in some questionable tactics which left a bad taste in Carter's mouth.

Carter then spread the word of Kyle's deviousness to other members of the community. Over time, no one would work with Kyle. This increased the work involved in Kyle's caseload, decreased his profit margin, and made it difficult for him to attain positive results for his clients. Kyle's lack of integrity excluded him from being "in" the workers' compensation community and while the "social sanctioning" did not immediately change Kyle's behavior, it did prevent him from attaining many successes in the workers' compensation field.

As the previous example reveals, social sanctioning can be an effective way of limiting the power and prestige of those who violate the ethical norms and values of a community. In some instances, it may even be effective to coerce compliance with generally accepted values inherent in the social contract.

On July 18, 2020, the United Nations Secretary-General António Guterres commented that

> the response to the pandemic, and to the widespread discontent that preceded it, must be based on a New Social Contract and a New Global Deal that create equal opportunities for all and respect the rights and freedoms of all.[12]

The social contract, as a heuristic for defining the role of government and individual rights, has evolved over time. From the seventeenth-century Hobbesian notions of an all-powerful sovereign to contemporary times, the views have changed, and the implicit and explicit agreements of peoples have evolved over time. The legal profession in the United States must itself consider whether a new social contract is merited – a contract which shuns those who abuse the system for self-gain and excludes those who utilize the power and status given to attorneys to harm others. Shifting the social contract for legal professionals involves overcoming common rationalizations.

Rationalizations in Practice

Attorneys are regularly faced with a variety of rationalizations which are sometimes used on a post hoc basis to justify unprofessional behavior, and at other times are used to convince oneself or another to engage in questionable activities, or to fail to speak or act when others do. Gentile distinguishes between "preemptive" and "real-time" rationalizations.[13] Preemptive rationalizations include those types of things that would stop us before we even start to voice values.[14] For instance, after witnessing something unethical, one may think "I don't have all the information," or "it's probably not worth addressing."[15] In the above example, Jamie faced and overcame preemptive rationalizations when almost refusing to help Scott. These types of rationalizations prevent us from acting before we even begin. Real-time rationalizations, on the other hand, are the kinds of things we expect people to say in response to certain values issues.[16] Gentile identifies four common types of real-time rationalizations, as outlined in Table 9.1.[17]

Table 9.1 Common Rationalizations

Common Rationalization	Example of Rationalization
Expected or Standard Practice	"Everyone does this, so it's really standard practice. It's even expected."
Materiality	"The impact of this action is not material. It doesn't really hurt anyone."
Locus of Responsibility	"This is not my responsibility; I'm just following orders here."
Locus of Loyalty	"I know this isn't quite fair to the customer but I don't want to hurt my reports/team/boss/company."

These rationalizations are common in business and legal practice. They are sometimes used as a means of attempting to make oneself feel better about engaging in actions one knows one should not engage in, or to stop action before it even begins or after it is initiated. In some instances, these rationalizations are used to try to convince another to engage in questionable activities. Gentile suggests focusing on how to respond to these arguments so when one is faced with a rationalization-based argument in practice, one is prepared to respond to it. Table 9.2 summarizes Gentile's proposed considerations for analyzing and overcoming each category of rationalization.[18]

Table 9.2 Overcoming Common Rationalizations

Rationalization	Proposed Considerations
Standard Practice ("Everyone does it")	This is often an exaggeration and one should query into the consequences for trust, why there might be laws or policies against it, one's comfort level if others became aware one was doing it, etc.
Materiality ("It's a small thing")	One should recognize the ambiguous nature of materiality and how it is measured, as well as how some practices are simply fraudulent no matter how small. And if it's "small" then this will be the easiest time to address it before it becomes much larger and more costly – but necessary – to do so.
Locus of Responsibility ("It's not my job")	This is an acknowledgment that someone doesn't like what is happening here, and this opens an opportunity for discussion, which may involve one's fear of consequences for non-compliance. This opens the door for creative problem solving and positioning oneself as helping to avoid risk.
Locus of Loyalty ("I owe it to my boss")	One should consider that there are many ways that loyalty can be framed, including loyalty to the long-term interests of the company and its reputation.

The legal field contains many attorneys who simply accept the way things are or an authority figure's instructions without questioning whether their actions and proposed justifications are worthy of credence. In the following example, Mia was tasked with overcoming her own and her supervisor's rationalizations.

THE BILLING ERROR

Mia was an associate attorney who was, among other things, responsible for keeping track of her billable hours in six (6) minute increments. For any part of a six (6) minute period she worked, she was required to input .1 of an hour in the firm's billing software. If Mia worked 1 to 6 minutes, she would bill .1 of an hour. If Mia worked 7–12 minutes, she would bill .2 of an hour, and so on in like six minute increments until an hour is reached. This was the standard billing practice in Mia's state and the endorsed billing practice of the state's bar association.

Mia would enter her hours in the firm's billing software every day. The office staff then mailed monthly invoices to each client reflecting the time Mia and others in the firm spent on each case, along with the current balance of each client. One day Mia meant to enter .4 of an hour into the firm's billing software for legal research she conducted. However, because of a missed keystroke, she instead entered four hours of time for the legal research. Mia didn't notice the error until months later when the case was approaching settlement and long after the invoice had been mailed to and paid for by the client.

This one little input error led to the client being billed over a thousand dollars more than the client should have been billed for the research Mia conducted. When she noticed the error she wasn't sure what to do. No one else noticed her mistake, the client had already paid, and Mia also was required to reach her minimum number of billable hours each year, so her error would help her reach her quota faster. She, however, didn't feel good about charging a client so much for so little, and so approached her supervising attorney about what she should do.

Her supervising attorney responded to "ignore it and be more careful next time," and that "this is pretty minor, especially for a client so rich ... it's like pennies to him." Anyway, he said, "there's no way the client could know how long you spent on research" and "the client has already paid."

While Mia was somewhat relieved by her supervisor's response, she still didn't feel good about it and so suggested to him that she understood but still that she "didn't think it was fair to the client to be overbilled" because of her mistake, and that she "still had some work to do on his case," and suggested that she "bill only .4 of an hour for the next 4 hours" she worked on the case. Her supervisor agreed and said they would also note the credit and correction on the client's next invoice.

In the previous example, Mia was able to overcome the immateriality rationalization by devising a strategy for correcting a billing error her supervisor didn't think was significant. Mia subsequently realized that her supervisor wasn't committed to defrauding the client but didn't want to deal with the issue or refund the client's money. By proposing an alternative solution that conformed to generally accepted values, Mia was able to change her supervisor's mind and correct the error. In the next example, consider how April and her colleagues were able to effectuate values while overcoming the locus of loyalty rationalization.

THE RESPECTED COLLEAGUE

April was a partner in a medium-sized firm. Leonard, the most senior partner in the firm, mentored April early in her career, provided her with helpful advice over the years, assisted her with retaining new clients, and was very well-respected within her firm and the legal community. Leonard was approaching retirement and was simultaneously having some health issues. He was nonetheless widely regarded as the firm's best attorney and was very knowledgeable and cared about by everyone in the firm. Everyone in the firm, including April, had gratitude for Leonard's mentoring, the example he set, and his calm and caring nature.

Over time, Leonard reduced his caseload as part of his planned transition into retirement and handed off many of his cases and clients to April and other attorneys in the firm. In one of the cases that Leonard had started and was handed over to April, she noticed that Leonard had overlooked some recent case law which would undermine the arguments he was trying to make. Leonard hadn't been keeping up on recent developments like he used to. He lacked the energy and initiative he once had. The new case law was detrimental to the case, and the clients were never informed of it. April's evaluation led her to believe that the case was almost certain to be dismissed.

April was conflicted between her loyalty to Leonard and her responsibilities to her client and court. She also didn't want Leonard or the firm to be sued for malpractice, which would be a probable consequence of continuing to pursue this case. April wanted to ask Leonard about it, but he was on vacation in Hawaii visiting his son and had made clear that he didn't want to be bothered while traveling. As a result, she brought some of the other partners of the firm into the conversation. The other partners agreed that the case would be dismissed yet simultaneously felt loyalty to Leonard. They didn't want to hurt his reputation or standing in the community by undermining what he had told the clients, so they worked together to develop a strategy that would simultaneously protect Leonard's reputation, the firm, and the client's interests.

The partners decided to write up a memorandum of law which incorporated the new case law and explained, for the clients, how the firm's prior evaluation of the case was based on the law existing prior to these changes and, after these changes to the law, there was little chance of success.

The partners then looped Leonard into the conversation upon his return from Hawaii and gave him the opportunity to present the memorandum to the client himself. Leonard then set up a meeting and explained the situation to the client. Leonard followed up the meeting by sending the client the memorandum along with a letter refunding the client's retainer fee.

The partners were able to successfully strategize to remain loyal to their long-time mentor, Leonard by giving him the chance to correct his mistake himself thereby protecting his reputation while ensuring loyalty to the firm and client's interests.

As the previous example illustrates, overcoming common rationalizations often requires creative strategies. It may involve questioning commonly accepted practices and purported justifications for those practices. Rationalizations may arise and be overcome through individual conversations with others, developing new practices within a firm, or even through the development of or appeals to extant social contracts (ESCs) within an organization or community.

Extant Social Contracts

Beyond the social contract between the legal field and society, there co-exist a multitude of ESCs that impact attorneys in the legal field.[19] As Dunfee explains

ESCs are existing social contracts embodying actual behavioral norms which derive from shared goals, beliefs and attitudes of groups or communities of people. The ESCs are typically informal agreements and are generally not reduced to a definitive set of words. Although the agreements may be express they would more commonly be implied from certain characteristics, attitudes and patterns of the group. In some instances, for example joining a professional organization, there would be direct evidence of consent to the ESC.[20]

The ESC concept involves a person's consent to implicit or explicit agreements about how one should behave within a community, organization, firm, or other institution. An attorney may find, for instance, that the norms which are shared in a religious organization are not the same as the norms of the legal field or a law firm. Deciphering a way to reconcile incoherent ESCs and the behavioral norms that derive from them is the cause of many ethical dilemmas. Christianity teaches compassion and kindness as the appropriate behavioral norms, but in an adversarial setting, in one's role as an advocate, an attorney must sometimes be abrasive in the face of an adversary. Such conflicts of norms make some attorneys uncomfortable in the role of an advocate.

ESCs may be formed intentionally among a group of people to develop a shared way of dealing with given situations. Business codes of conduct are one form of an intentionally developed ESC that is aimed at guiding the behaviors of employees of a business. Various organizations also develop similar codes which are intended to guide the behavior of members of the organizations. The professional rules themselves may be viewed as an ESC. However, not all ESCs are as explicit. At times, ESCs may be a function of the unwritten but accepted practices of a court, jurisdiction, or other community. Many ESCs arise as implied understandings of the way people should interact in a situation. As the following example illustrates, one may utilize ESCs as a strategy for voicing values.

SENDING A MESSAGE

In litigation, extensions of time to file an Answer to a Complaint are regularly agreed to between counsel. It is a common courtesy extended to defense counsel. Agreeing to such an extension of time comes with the understanding that the plaintiff's counsel may at some point in the litigation need this courtesy reciprocated for extensions in responding to discovery or other deadlines. Such extensions are not required to be agreed to by court rules, but attorneys regularly provide this courtesy to each other with the expectation that the courtesy will be reciprocated.

After a failed mediation, Sonia filed a Complaint and the defense requested that Sonia agree to an extension to Answer the Complaint. Under normal circumstances, Sonia would not hesitate to extend the standard courtesy. However, in this instance she felt as though she was misled and used by defense counsel. The mediation itself was a waste of time and Sonia's firm expended over 10,000 dollars on mediation fees to only be "played" by the defense who used the opportunity to gather more information and prepare their defenses. The defense offered Sonia's firm no possibility of resolution during the mediation, aka, they did not even make a settlement offer. Sonia was livid after this failed mediation particularly because she was led to believe that there was potential for resolution when there was none, the clients were upset saying that the defense was already "kicking their butts," and the firm expended valuable resources on a bad faith mediation.

While Sonia would normally agree to an extension of time to answer, she felt as though agreeing in this instance would be akin to "taking another kick in the face." She therefore declined to offer the standard extension as a matter of principle, and explained her rationale to defense counsel, and that they violated the shared understanding that mediation was to take place in good faith. While Sonia had little doubt that a judge would grant defense counsel's motion to extend the time to answer, which the defense was surely going to file because she did not consent, she felt a message needed to be sent to defense counsel that their bad faith actions were unacceptable.

In the preceding example, Sonia was subject to bad faith and the victim of a violation of the ESC that mediations be entered into in good faith and so she felt it necessary to voice this by not cooperating with the defense counsel on a matter of common courtesy and explaining her reasoning for doing so. She was able to utilize her refusing to participate in a commonly accepted ESC (agreeing to the extension) to send a message to the defense that their violation of another ESC (engaging in mediation in good faith) was not acceptable.

Integrative Social Contracts Theory

Integrative Social Contracts Theory ("ISCT") provides a framework for determining how to reconcile conflicting ESCs and norms within and across cultures, organizations, firms, communities, and other institutions.[21] While most lawyers would not be inclined to utilize the methods and processes of ISCT on a regular basis, it is utilized here to show instrumentally

that the common rationalization of the "business decision" is a violation of
the social contract or, in other words, ISCT is utilized to show that attorneys
who attempt to justify immoral behavior based solely on business or profitability are violating the social contract. The ISCT decision-making process is
outlined in Figure 9.1.[22]

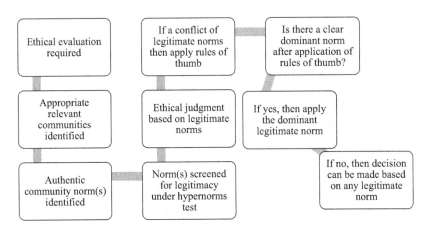

Figure 9.1 ISCT Decision-Making Process

While a full explanation of the ISCT process is beyond the scope of this
chapter, suffice it to say that utilizing ISCT reveals that the "business decision" norm violates the social contract. The first step to the ISCT decision-
making process is to recognize that ethical evaluation is necessary. Once
that is done, the next step is to identify relevant communities, which is
defined broadly to include law firms, the legal field, and a variety of other
institutions. Then, one should identify the community norms that do exist
in these communities that would be applicable to a given situation. Here,
there is the "business decision" norm, which is one authentic community norm within the legal field. This norm, however, would not pass the
"hypernorms" screening test, because it would allow one to harm others
by infringing upon their rights to life, liberty, and property. As a result,
the norm of the "business decision" cannot be deemed a legitimate norm
within the ISCT framework, and so following that norm would be a violation of the societal (macro) social contract.

Gentile discusses how the language of ISCT, and particularly "hypernorms" may be instrumental in finding shared values when an ethical issue
arises.[23] Hypernorms represent those values that are shared across peoples
and cultures – they are the core values of humanity at a given point in time.

THE BUSINESS OF LAW AND COMMON RATIONALIZATIONS

If a values conflict rises to the level of hypernorms, then those involved may more easily find common ground to communicate despite their differences. On the other hand, the list of values that rise to hypernorms is a short list. This list may include not only basic human rights and human dignity, but also integrity, justice, and compassion.[24] These are values shared across most people regardless of the community they belong to or cultural differences. Beyond hypernorms, many values are more local, that is, they are based on experience, culture, religion, or family backgrounds. These types of values may not be shared across general populations. Some values are conventional or even matters of personal preference, comfort, and style.

ISCT is particularly useful for deciphering situations when two authentic norms come into conflict with each other. For instance, the "helping one's friends" norm may come into conflict with the "do what's best for the firm" norm, when one is asked to represent a friend for a lower cost than one could otherwise attain if putting time and effort into another client's case.[25] Such conflicts regularly arise in firm contexts, and it is not uncommon for friends to attempt to solicit free legal advice or reduced cost services from attorneys. ISCT provides another lens by which one can view one's obligations under the social contract and reveals that the extreme version of uninhibited profit-seeking, as represented in the "business decision" norm, does not withstand scrutiny.

Overcoming Rationalizations and Modifying the Social Contract

The practice of law is infused with ESCs among individuals, among organizations, and among individuals and organizations. The political connections and affiliations of attorneys influence who they are willing to deal with, settle cases with, and work with. Friendships and relationships matter within the social contract; often those relationships are long-lasting and evolve over time.[26] Common sense dictates that human are more willing to work with those they trust, those they have institutional relationships with, or those with whom they share common viewpoints.

In contemporary times, parody has become a tool for normalizing the illegitimate norms associated with the legal field and politics. Societal members are quick to crack a joke about corruption in the system and widely accept that self-interest guides many political decisions. While many have contempt for these realities, not everyone takes action to effectuate change.

The social contract deteriorates when the population's apathetic complacency permits corruption and cronyism to continue at the highest levels of law and government.

Modifying the social contract involves moving beyond the normalization of corruption, unbridled profit-seeking, and rationalizations of these practices as "just the way things are." Yet, when one is in the inner circle of cronyism, one would not likely suggest there is anything wrong with it. When one benefits from a practice, one tends to support it absent some overriding reason for rejecting the practice. Similarly, so long as attorneys continue to benefit from viewing the profession through the lens of profit motivations, absent some overriding reason to reject the practice, some will likely continue it. Surely those attorneys who fall on the "opportunistic" side of the bell curve will continue this practice. However, most people (yes, attorneys are people too) are not purely opportunistic but fall somewhere on the curve of the bell. Most have the ability to view the legal profession as something more than a profit-center. Consider the following example.

THAT'S JUST THE WAY IT IS

Teresa worked as a senior associate at a law firm well known for being a cut-throat environment, where those high up were known for "pulling out the weeds" instead of "watering every plant." The firm offered little training for new attorneys and no formal mentoring. The firm had high employee turn-over rates and the firm was more often than most firms sued by former employees and clients. Simultaneously, the firm offered very high associate salaries, prestige, and high annual bonuses.

Teresa worked hard throughout her entire life to get into the best schools, to graduate at the top of her law school class, and to land her high paying associate position. She valued money and material possessions above all else, would often buy expensive purses and clothes to flaunt them to make other women jealous. She thrived in toxic environments, she herself being toxic, and would, without even recognizing that she was harming others, manipulate and use people to advance her career. Teresa was raised to believe that manipulation was normal. She couldn't recognize normal social boundaries or conform her behavior to the ethical norms of society. Some might say she had a personality disorder, but it was never diagnosed. Regardless, she lacked empathy for others and acted only to advance her own interests.

When Julie joined the firm as a junior associate, she was assigned to work with Teresa to facilitate a complex business transaction. Julie identified a new way of facilitating the transaction which would immediately save the client a large amount of money and would continue to save the client money year-over-year. Julie brought this idea to Teresa who initially rejected Julie's proposal and then, after shutting Julie down, had a call with the client, and explained the concept. The client loved the idea and Teresa was attributed all the credit from the client and within the firm. Teresa gladly accepted all praise and did not attribute any credit to Julie.

Julie was furious that Teresa stole her idea and claimed credit for it. She approached Teresa about it first and Teresa lied to Julie saying, that she was already exploring the idea before Julie approached her and made an underhanded comment snarking "that's just the way it is." As a relatively new junior associate Julie was surprised by Teresa's dishonesty and opportunism. Julie felt powerless to do anything about it. Based on her conversation with Teresa, Julie feared that if she voiced the issue Teresa would lie about it and she further feared that no one would believe her over Teresa.

Despite her fear, Julie refused to accept that Teresa's actions were acceptable and refused to accept her assessment that "that's just the way it is." However, Julie recognized that it was not then the right time to act. She had no way of proving that Teresa stole her idea and took credit for it. Instead of acting at that moment, Julie decided to document the issue (but not send it to anyone), continue building allies within the firm, and wait for a future opportunity to make change.

As the previous example illustrates, when one is faced with sheer opportunism, it creates difficult issues. Opportunists are often incapable of seeing the wrong in their actions or how they harm others. They are incapable of overcoming deep-seated rationalizations. It often takes patience and long-term strategies, such as building allies and waiting for the right time, to deal with opportunists. One must further be cautious not to buy into their flawed rationalizations.

Overcoming rationalizations is particularly challenging because it is "frightening to think and painful to change" and overcoming rationalizations will typically only "occur incrementally and over a long period of time."[27] Embedding virtues and values into the education, profession, and practice of law may over time contribute to overcoming such rationalizations. Ethics education should coincide with modifying institutions and incentives, so that the "business decision" rationalization is no longer perceived to be acceptable. Financial incentives may be aligned with ethics goals to motivate attorneys to question common rationalizations and move beyond them. Strategies for voicing values may be practiced and utilized so that attorneys have the confidence and skill set needed to move beyond such rationalizations and act on their values.

Reconciling Financial Needs (and Wants) with Ethical Practices

Self-interest remains at the heart of many ethical quandaries. While it is easy to posit a general assertion that financial incentives should align with ethics goals, the implementation of how this could be done needs further examination. The crux of the issue is that aligning financial needs with ethical goals will only do so much because many have financial wants that far exceed their needs. While basic needs may be aligned with ethical action, some people will always be willing to risk unethical action to attain significant financial rewards particularly when the risk of being caught or sanctioned is low. There will always be some who are willing to be unethical to make money. There will always be some who do it successfully and without getting caught. Simultaneously, there will always be some who strive to be good people who are also financially successful.

The legitimate needs of the members of the legal profession must be met within a social contract that rejects rationalizations based in extreme notions of the "business decision," while allowing attorneys to flourish within their practices, and to shun members of the legal community whose actions contribute to the deterioration of the reputation of the profession. The route to ensuring ethical action in the practice of law must be navigated by ensuring that attorneys in practice have sufficient financial resources so that they can afford to stand on their principles without concern for where their next meal will come from. While some will always attempt unethical action for even more money (the "opportunists"), the rest of the profession, if in a stable financial position, will be better equipped to socially sanction such attorneys as they, over time, become more and more the outliers of the legal profession.

It is all too easy to accept that ethics may be ignored because of insufficient income. While financial struggles may be an explanation for some unethical actions, it should not be rationalized to be a socially acceptable reason for engaging in unethical acts. Consider the following example of how insufficient income can lead to rationalizations.

I DON'T MAKE ENOUGH MONEY

Tim took a position at a small firm as a law clerk while he was trying to pass the bar exam. He was paid a little above minimum wage and was told that when he passed the bar, he would get a pay increase and become an associate attorney with the firm. Tim had already failed the bar exam once and had to wait until the next year to take it again. In the meantime, Tim continued to work as a law clerk. He was upset because he had a law degree, had invested all that time and money in law school, and still wasn't getting paid much.

Tim needed office supplies to continue his studies for the bar exam. He couldn't spare much money to buy office supplies, so he took them from the law office without permission. He said to himself, "If I was getting paid more, I wouldn't need to take them," and rationalized his stealing by thinking that "the law office can afford it, I can't."

Over the months that followed, Tim continued to take supplies from the office, until one day Shae, the office manager, saw him put some supplies in his bag. The cost of supplies had increased in recent months, and Shae couldn't explain why it had increased to the firm's owners. Upon seeing Tim put some supplies in his bag, she had a probable explanation for the cost increase.

Shae reported what she saw to the firm's owners. The next week, Tim was terminated from employment for stealing. While he was able to rationalize the theft in his own mind, others saw things very differently.

As the previous example illustrates, one's rationalizations for unethical acts are often internal attempts at justifying unethical actions. When thought about from the perspective of others, many rationalizations, such as "they can afford it" are not worthy of credence.

Ethics education coinciding with reasonable pay, adequate benefits, and a comfortable quality of life for members of the legal profession can contribute to improving the social contract and overcoming common rationalizations. At the heart of the legal profession's social contract is society granting lawyers not only respect and autonomy, but also financial rewards in exchange for attorneys providing professional and ethical representation of public and private rights. Without adequate attorney compensation for ethical and professional work, attorneys may have an excuse, but certainly not a justification, for acting unethically. Such rationalizations should be carefully guarded against, and institutions should work to align financial incentives with ethical actions so that the many lawyers who exist on the bell curve can easier align the core values of advocates with successful careers in the legal field. Until such institutional change takes place, however, the GVV methodologies provide many tools that attorneys can use to recognize and overcome rationalizations, and strategies for voicing change so that members of the legal profession can fulfill their part of the social contract by providing competent, professional, and ethical representation of the interests of private citizens and the public.

The social contract provides another lens by which to examine a lawyer's moral obligations and another useful tool for analyzing what lawyers owe to each other and society. Social contract theory provides a mechanism for determining which norms withstand the hypernorm legitimacy test. Some of the norms that are accepted simply as a matter of course like the "business decision" rationalization may not, in fact, be legitimate norms. Such norms need to give way to other legitimate norms that better cohere with existing ethical constructs. The GVV methodology provides strategies for challenging illegitimate norms, for prioritizing legitimate norms, for overcoming rationalizations, and for effectuating values and the central tenets of the social contract within the legal field.

Notes

1 Thomas Donaldson, *Corporations and Morality*, 40–41 (1982).
2 Thomas Hobbes, *Leviathan* (1651); John Locke, *Two Treatises of Government* (1689); Jean-Jacques Rousseau, *The Social Contract* (1762); Jean-Jacques Rousseau, *Discourse on Inequality* (1755).
3 Anita L. Allen, Social Contract Theory in American Case Law, 51 *Fla. L. Rev.* 1, 3–5 (1999).
4 Visit Monticello today and the portrait is still hanging.

5 John Locke, *Two Treatises of Government* (1689); *United States Declaration of Independence* (1776).

6 J.W. Gough, *The Social Contract*, 229–243 (1936).

7 Sylvia R. Cruess and Richard L. Cruess, Professionalism and Medicine's Social Contract with Society, 6 *Virtual Mentor* 185 (2004) (identifying a similar social contract for physicians).

8 Edward Freeman et al., *Stakeholder Theory: The State of the Art* (2010), 222 (The separation thesis provides that "The discourse of business and the discourse of ethics can be separated so that sentences like 'x is a business decision' have no moral content, and 'x is a moral decision' have no business content"); see also Edward Freeman, The Politics of Stakeholder Theory: Some Future Directions, 4 *Business Ethics Quarterly* 409, 412 (1994).

9 Mary Gentile, *Ethical Leadership through Giving Voice to Values*, Coursera Course.

10 *Id.*

11 *Id.*

12 United Nations, *Tackling Inequality: A New Social Contract for a New Era*, https://www.un.org/sustainabledevelopment/a-new-social-contract-for-a-new-era/

13 Mary Gentile, *Ethical Leadership through Giving Voice to Values*, Coursera Course.

14 *Id.*

15 *Id.*

16 *Id.*

17 Mary Gentile, *Giving Voice to Values: How to Counter Rationalizations Rationally* (October 10, 2017), https://ideas.darden.virginia.edu/giving-voice-to-values-how-to-counter-rationalizations-rationally

18 *Id.* (Table 9.1 is drawn from Gentile's text).

19 See Thomas Donaldson and Thomas Dunfee, *The Ties That Bind: A Social Contracts Approach to Business Ethics* (1999); and Thomas Dunfee, Business Ethics and Extant Social Contracts, 1 *Business Ethics Quarterly* 23 (1991).

20 Thomas Dunfee, Business Ethics and Extant Social Contracts, 1 *Business Ethics Quarterly* 23, 32 (1991).

21 See generally Thomas Donaldson and Thomas Dunfee, *The Ties That Bind: A Social Contracts Approach to Business Ethics* (1999).

22 *Id.* at 206. (author's adaptation).

23 Mary Gentile, *Ethical Leadership through Giving Voice to Values*, Coursera Course.

24 *Id.*

25 For an analysis of this conflict of norms within the social contract framework, see Keith William Diener, *Multi-layered Integrative Social Contracts Theory (MISCT): A Contractualist Framework for Business Ethics*, Georgetown University Doctoral Dissertation (2014).

26 Steven McGill, *A Hurdler's Hurdler: The Life of Rodney Milburn, Olympic Champion* (2018); David Fajgenbaum, *Chasing My Cure: A Doctor's Race to Turn Hope into Action* (2019).

27 Neel Burton, Self-deception I: Rationalization; Human Beings Are Not Rational, But Rationalizing Animals, *Psychology Today* (updated May 4, 2020), https://www.psychologytoday.com/us/blog/hide-and-seek/201203/self-deception-i-rationalization

CONCLUSION

This book suggests that business ethics theory, including the tenets of *Giving Voice to Values*, provides many insights into how lawyers may better identify, analyze, and act upon values in the legal field.

Part I traced the historical development of the contemporary common law legal system. It described salient environmental factors that influence ethics in the legal field. It began in Chapter 1 by tracing the history of the common law to decipher the historical roots of norms in legal practice and revealed that the legal field has a history fraught with practices that deviate from general societal norms. It showed that the contemporary legal landscape in the United States is a product of over a millennium of historical events that have created an imperfect institution for administering justice. It discussed how the U.S. system diverged in many ways from its English roots as it began to develop many of its own legal norms that deviated from its birth mother. Chapter 2 examined how the American Rule on the recovery of attorneys' fees, one such norm, influenced the evolution of the practice of law in the United States including the progression of entrepreneurial

litigation. It examined the way that the rules and standard employed by
U.S. courts has had a tremendous impact on practitioners. Chapter 3 examined the impact of the economy on the practice of law and how broader
socio-economic trends impacted and influenced the practice of law and the
motivations and needs of attorneys. Part I described the central aspects of
the external political and economic systems within which attorneys in the
United States are currently working and how this system influences ethical
decision making.

With the broader context of the external environment set forth, Part II
turned to the individual legal practitioner who works in the contemporary legal environment. Chapter 4 examined the role of the attorney as an
advocate and the core values of advocacy. These values were defined and
explored in the context of the adversarial setting of the practice of law. The
strategies of Giving Voice to Values were examined and implemented to decipher
ways of expressing values effectively in legal contexts. Chapter 5 turned to
the attorney's challenge of building trust with stakeholders and adapted
Fort's tripartite vision of trust to the practice of law. It emphasized that
developing trust with clients and other stakeholders is a key component of
effective advocacy. Following the examination of trust, Chapter 6 investigated the unethical employer and firm environment. It provided an outline
of a framework for subordinates desiring to address unethical and unprofessional conduct of their superiors in firm settings. Part II examined the
attorney's role as an advocate and how that role can be enhanced by adherence to values.

Having considered the external environment and the role of the attorney
as an advocate, Part III delved deeper into ways that attorneys can effectively
voice their values in legal practice by moving beyond the strict letter of the
rules of professional conduct. Chapter 7 examined the professional rules
and how values play a role in promoting ethical action beyond mere compliance. Chapter 8 adapted the stakeholder concept from business ethics
literature to the legal profession and discussed how the concept and theory
may provide both instrumental and normative insights to legal practitioners. Chapter 9 considered that law has business components that cannot be
separated from people and ethics. It suggested that the social contract needs
to be modified to exclude extreme profit-seeking motivations from the
legal field, and that embedding virtues and values into the education, profession, and practice of law, and implementing the strategies of Giving Voice

to *Values* will over time contribute to overcoming rationalizations. Part III called for attorneys to look to and beyond the model rules when making practice decisions.

The adversarial nature of the common law system, the array of rules and standards of the legal field, and external socio-economic factors all combine to set the stage for unique and often complex ethical challenges for lawyers. The three parts of this book combine to form an introductory guide to how the theory and principles of business ethics, including the tenets of *Giving Voice to Values*, may be utilized to improve ethical decision making in the legal field. While no single book can provide a comprehensive framework for addressing every situation that may arise, this book contributes to the field of law by providing practical guidance and the theoretical underpinning of that guidance, and by helping lawyers have the tools they need to make, communicate, and effectuate ethically sound decisions in legal contexts.

INDEX

Note: **Bold** page numbers refer to tables, *italic* page numbers refer to figures and page numbers followed by "n" refer to end notes.

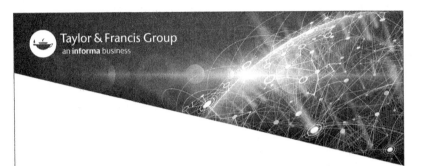

Printed in the United States
by Baker & Taylor Publisher Services